T0271113

Risk Management Maturity

Crises like the COVID-19 pandemic are wake-up calls for enterprises to review their current risk management models. This book suggests a more robust risk management maturity model and illustrates the application in crisis situations.

The book surveys existing risk management maturity models and proposes a new model appropriate for assessing the risk management processes in enterprises during times of crisis. Its key advantages include the correlation of its attributes with crisis situations and an innovative methodological approach to model development. The authors use the model to examine 107 enterprises from the financial services, construction and IT sector, showing how it allows the user to identify risk management maturity changes in the aftermath of the COVID-19 pandemic.

The book will interest entrepreneurs, managers and risk management professionals, who can use the model in their management processes, as well as enterprise stakeholders and academics.

Sylwia Bąk holds a PhD in Management Sciences. She is Assistant Professor and works as Researcher and Lecturer in the Management Systems Department of Jagiellonian University in Krakow, Poland. In her interests, research and publications, she focuses on issues related to risk management, crisis management, strategic management and standardized management systems.

Piotr Jedynak is Professor of Management. He works at Jagiellonian University in Krakow, Poland, where he holds the positions of Vice-Rector for Financial and HR Policy and Head of the Management Systems Department. He specializes in risk management, strategic management and management systems. He is the author of numerous publications, an auditor and consultant to many public and business organizations.

Routledge Focus on Business and Management

The fields of business and management have grown exponentially as areas of research and education. This growth presents challenges for readers trying to keep up with the latest important insights. *Routledge Focus on Business and Management* presents small books on big topics and how they intersect with the world of business research.

Individually, each title in the series provides coverage of a key academic topic, whilst collectively, the series forms a comprehensive collection across the business disciplines.

The Innovative Management Education Ecosystem
Reskilling and Upskilling the Future Workforce
Jordi Diaz, Daphne Halkias and Paul W. Thurman

Management and Labor Conflict
An Introduction to the US and Canadian History
Jason Russell

Creativity, Innovation and the Fourth Industrial Revolution
The da Vinci Strategy
Jon-Arild Johannessen

Performance Measurement in Non-Profit Organizations
The Road to Integrated Reporting
Patrizia Gazzola and Stefano Amelio

Risk Management Maturity
A Multidimensional Model
Sylwia Bąk and Piotr Jedynak

For more information about this series, please visit: www.routledge.com/Routledge-Focus-on-Business-and-Management/book-series/FBM

Risk Management Maturity

A Multidimensional Model

Sylwia Bąk and Piotr Jedynak

Routledge
Taylor & Francis Group

LONDON AND NEW YORK

First published 2023
by Routledge
4 Park Square, Milton Park, Abingdon, Oxon OX14 4RN

and by Routledge
605 Third Avenue, New York, NY 10158

Routledge is an imprint of the Taylor & Francis Group, an informa business

British Library Cataloguing-in-Publication Data
A catalogue record for this book is available from the British Library

Library of Congress Cataloging-in-Publication Data
Names: Bąk, Sylwia, author. | Jedynak, Piotr, author.
Title: Risk management maturity : a multidimensional model /
Sylwia Bąk and Piotr Jedynak.
Description: New York, NY : Routledge, 2023. |
Series: Routledge focus on business and management |
Includes bibliographical references and index. |
Identifiers: LCCN 2022032650 (print) | LCCN 2022032651 (ebook) |
ISBN 9781032362366 (hardback) | ISBN 9781032362380 (paperback) |
ISBN 9781003330905 (ebook)
Subjects: LCSH: Risk management. | Risk management–
Auditing. | Auditing, Internal.
Classification: LCC HD61 .B3523 2023 (print) | LCC HD61 (ebook) |
DDC 659.2–dc23/eng/20220907
LC record available at https://lccn.loc.gov/2022032650
LC ebook record available at https://lccn.loc.gov/2022032651

ISBN: 9781032362366 (hbk)
ISBN: 9781032362380 (pbk)
ISBN: 9781003330905 (ebk)

DOI: 10.4324/9781003330905

Typeset in Times New Roman
by Newgen Publishing UK

Contents

Figures

Tables

Preface

Due to our perceived need to reflect on the impact of crisis situations on risk management maturity, in this book, we review and discuss the existing risk management maturity models with regard to the specifics of risk management in crisis situations. We want to propose a new, reconstructed model that is more appropriate for measuring risk management maturity in companies experiencing crises.

The key advantages of our model include the correlation of its attributes with crisis situations, the innovative methodological approach to model development and the application of a special procedure aimed to validate proposed model and test its applicability during the crisis following the COVID-19 pandemic. The adopted approach to model validation allows us to identify changes that occurred in the risk management maturity of the 107 examined enterprises in the aftermath of the COVID-19 pandemic.

The main objective of the book is to familiarize the reader with a new approach to measuring risk management maturity. After reading it, the reader should have basic theoretical knowledge of the impact of crisis situations on risk management maturity as well as practical skills relating to the possibility and methods of using the model in assessing the maturity of risk management processes implemented in an enterprise.

The essence of the book, therefore, is to support enterprises in their pursuit of better risk management processes by providing them with a new measurement tool that can be used in different operating conditions, including crises. The book is addressed to entrepreneurs, managers and risk management professionals, who can use our model and other information included in the book in their management processes, as well as stakeholders of various enterprises, the business and academia communities and students of all levels.

Sylwia Bąk and Piotr Jedynak

Credits

The publication was funded by the Priority Research Area Society of the Future under the programme 'Excellence Initiative – Research University' at the Jagiellonian University in Krakow.

Introduction

Based on the results of our previous research on risk management challenges and problems faced by numerous companies from different sectors during the COVID-19 pandemic, we saw the need to reflect on the adequacy of the existing risk management maturity models for crisis situations such as the COVID-19 pandemic. Accordingly, in this book we attempt to review and discuss the existing risk management maturity models with regard to the specific requirements of risk management in crisis situations. We also want to propose a new, reconstructed model that is more appropriate for measuring risk management maturity in companies experiencing crises.

The primary objective of our book is to build a multidimensional model for assessing risk management maturity that is tailored to the specific demands of crisis situations and to validate this model in enterprises from several different sectors. The adopted approach to model validation allows us to identify changes that occurred in the risk management maturity of the examined enterprises in the aftermath of the COVID-19 pandemic. The examined enterprises represent the sectors of financial services, construction and IT. We compared the respective companies' risk management maturity in the two years: 2018 (the pre-pandemic period) and 2020 (a few months after the onset of the COVID-19 pandemic and during its course). Using a triangulation of research methods, we sought to answer the following questions: Did the COVID-19 pandemic change the level of risk management maturity in the enterprises under examination? If so, what was the character of these changes?

The objective of the first chapter is to review the existing models for assessing risk management maturity that we have identified in the academic literature. We present theoretical aspects of organizational risk management maturity and approaches to defining its levels. We present models for assessing risk management maturity as measuring

DOI: 10.4324/9781003330905-1

tools enabling a diagnosis of the level of advancement and development of risk management processes, indicating the target benchmark state, facilitating the identification of areas requiring improvement and stimulating the improvement of risk management in an enterprise. In this chapter we analyse in detail 34 models for assessing risk management maturity, developed between 1997 and 2021.

The objective of the second chapter is to identify the relationship between the occurrence of crisis situations and risk management maturity. Being aware that one of the most important circumstances strongly verifying the validity of the existing risk management systems and exposing their numerous imperfections are crises, in this chapter we show the characteristics of crises in the context of business activities and indicate their organizational, personal, technological, procedural, logistical, image-building and other implications. We also present the COVID-19 pandemic as a so far non-specific type of crisis experienced by enterprises and analyse its impact on the scope of identified risk factors and on enterprises' risk management systems. Lastly, we identify crises as an important argument for the measurement of risk management maturity and the development of a methodological approach to such measurement that would be adequate for the conditions created by crisis situations.

The goal of the third chapter is to present the methodology of the conducted empirical research. In this chapter we formulate research objectives and questions, define the stages of the conducted research process, develop a catalogue of methods and tools used in the research process and describe the data sources used in the research process. The main objective of our research was to build a model for assessing risk management maturity that would be adapted to the specifics of crisis situations such as the COVID-19 pandemic, to validate this model in enterprises from several different sectors and to establish a final diagnosis of how the COVID-19 pandemic had changed the level of risk management maturity in the enterprises under analysis.

The aim of the fourth chapter is to present our original risk management maturity assessment model, adapted to the specifics of crisis situations. Firstly, we present the procedure for developing a catalogue of eight attributes of our model, especially taking into account the risk management requirements applicable to crisis situations. For each of the eight attributes, we justify in detail the rationale for its inclusion in the model. Next we outline the process by which we developed the value scales for each attribute, emphasizing the importance of the rigour of the morphological analysis used in the process. The result of this activity was the development of the Morphological Matrix. In the last part of the chapter, we describe the process of developing an aggregate risk management maturity assessment scale taking into account the sum of points that the examined enterprises could receive as a result of the assessment of each attribute. Based on the developed assessment scale, we distinguished five levels of risk management maturity.

The aim of the fifth chapter is to present the procedure performed to validate our model on a sample of 107 enterprises. Using the developed model, we assessed the risk management maturity of examined enterprises representing the financial services, construction and IT sectors. The assessment was performed for two different periods, i.e. the years 2018 (the pre-pandemic period) and 2020 (several months after the onset of the COVID-19 pandemic and during its course). We present the detailed results of the scores obtained for individual attributes and the total scores constituting diagnoses of the risk management maturity of all examined enterprises in both periods.

The purpose of the sixth chapter is to present the results of our empirical research, i.e. to establish the impact of the COVID-19 pandemic on changes in the risk management maturity of the examined enterprises. We present the results of our analyses of the model's attributes in the case of which, in each of the studied sectors, the changes observed between 2018 and 2020 were so significant that they were reflected in their respective averaged (sectoral) scores. We looked for manifestations of the changes observed in their respective areas in the internal documentation of the analysed enterprises. The quotations from such source documents evidencing the aforementioned changes relating to the individual attributes were subjected to a qualitative content analysis using coding.

The goal of the seventh chapter is to present recommendations arising from the conclusions of the conducted empirical research and aimed at all types of business organizations (not only those covered by the research). We formulate our recommendations for those enterprises that wish to use our maturity model to measure and improve their risk management systems. Firstly, we present necessary organizational preparations for the risk management maturity assessment process to be conducted based on our model. We indicate participants in the assessment process and the methods of work organization within assessment teams. Furthermore, we discuss management implications resulting from our research regarding the integration of risk management maturity assessments with strategic management. We also provide information on the feasibility and scope of application of our model in different types of enterprises, diversified both geographically and sectorally.

1 Existing models for assessing risk management maturity

1.1 Risk management maturity

Organizational maturity is one of the most important concepts for measuring an organization's capabilities in various management areas. Maturity is understood as a measure of progress in demonstrating a particular capability or achieving a goal from the initial stage to the desired final outcome (Saleh, 2011). A maturity level is a defined, evolutionary state resulting from a process of continuous improvement. A manner of determining a level of maturity depends on the measurement tools used and their mutual synchronization (Haffer, 2011). Maturity models constitute typical examples of such tools. The use of models to assess maturity (competences, capabilities, a level of advancement) in the area of management (de Bruin et al., 2005) is based on the assumption that there exist relatively predictable and phased patterns of evolution of organizational changes which, when added together, indicate a path of logical consequences from the initial state to the state of full maturity (Pöppelbuß and Roglinger, 2011). Thus, a model of maturity can be seen as quantitatively or qualitatively presented stages of the increasing ability of specific attributes to achieve established objectives. A maturity model makes it possible to assess such attributes in defined areas and, in addition, allows for a systematic benchmarking analysis which is subsequently used as a basis for initiating an evaluative process of continuous improvement (Kwak and Ibbs, 2002; Fisher, 2004; Harmon, 2004; Kania, 2013).

In risk management, maturity refers to evolution towards the comprehensive development of risk management processes in an organization (RIMS, 2015). The use of maturity models dedicated to risk management started in the 1990s. In this case, maturity models serve, among other things, to develop intra-organizational risk management practices, focusing on assessing their effectiveness. They should

DOI: 10.4324/9781003330905-2

be closely adapted to the conditions in which risks can be identified, assessed and interpreted. Also, similarly to risk management standards, they are the result of a normative approach (Antonucci, 2016). The great importance of maturity models stems from the fact that, in order to shape effectively functioning risk management systems, they need to be assessed on a continuous basis with a view to identifying areas requiring improvement and showing possible directions of pursuing such improvement (Aven, 2016). Risk management maturity models (RMMM) enable such assessment. First of all, they make it possible to diagnose the level of sophistication and development of risk management processes and, moreover, indicate their model state (Chapman, 2011). They also support the identification of areas requiring improvement, stimulating the improvement of risk management processes and enabling the measurement of progress in improving risk management (Risk Management Research and Development Program Collaboration (RMRDPC), 2002; Schiller and Prpich 2014). They are therefore tools that can serve as benchmarks in both the process of implementing new risk management systems and the process of improving the existing systems (Jedynak and Bąk, 2018).

1.2 A comparison of the existing risk management maturity assessment models

1.2.1 The essence and applications of the models

So far, there have been dozens of proposals for RMMM. They are usually created by developing a catalogue of attributes (characteristic features to undergo assessment) and a maturity assessment scale adjusted to them. Such a scale should reflect the individual maturity levels of particular management practices in relation to the selected attributes and the overall subject of assessment. RMMM to date have the characteristics of either comprehensive models, in which case they are applied within a general risk management area, or functional models, in which case they are applied in selective management areas that directly or indirectly require the implementation of an approach to risk, such as project management, information security management, logistics or internal control (Jedynak and Bąk, 2018). After their initial construction, these models need to be updated regularly so that they remain adapted to the current situation of the organization, which, after all, is itself subject to constant change, both internally and in the sphere of relations with the environment.

6 Existing models for assessing risk management maturity

The model proposed by Hillson in 1997 (Hillson, 1997) is considered to be the first model dedicated to assessing the maturity of risk management. It was also a source of inspiration for the authors of subsequent maturity models. These models were usually presented and discussed individually; they were rarely the subjects of comparative reviews and analyses. The authors of comparative publications (cf. Zou et al., 2010; Wieczorek-Kosmala, 2014; Salawu and Abdullah, 2015; Caiadoa et al., 2016; Antonucci, 2016; Proença et al., 2017; Hoseini et al., 2019; Čech and Januška, 2020) tended to select up to a dozen, but usually a few, models. Consequently, such comparisons did not provide a complete picture of RMMM. The objective of this chapter is to review 34 models developed between 1997 and 2021, i.e. all known models that we have been able to identify in the literature on the subject. In comparing them, we used several criteria that allow for a preliminary recognition regarding both the structure of the models themselves and their possible applications (Table 1.1).

The models under analysis have individual authors or have been developed by professional organizations such as: International Association for Contract and Commercial Management (2003), Risk and Insurance Management Society (2006; 2015), Public Risk Management Association ALARM (2009), AON & Wharton School of the University of Pennsylvania (2011), IIRM Investors in Risk Management (2016), Deloitte (2016), Office of Rail and Road (2019) and OECD (2021).

Using the criterion of model type, we observed that the models always contained a set of attributes, i.e. characteristic features that should undergo assessment to provide the possibility of determining the level of advancement of risk management activities. In most cases, the sets of attributes were further supported by questionnaires, in which specific questions were formulated in such a way that answers to them should provide a full range of information allowing an assessment of each attribute.

Considering the criterion of target applications, the models under comparison can be divided into two groups: those that can be applied in general management and those dedicated to selected management areas such as project management (RMRDPC, 2002; Ren and Yeo, 2004, Yeo and Ren, 2009; Hopkinson and Lovelock, 2004; Loosemore et al., 2006; Öngel, 2009; Zou et al., 2010; Hopkinson, 2011; Salawu and Abdullah, 2015; Hoseini et al., 2019; Hartono et al., 2019), information security management (Lacey, 2007; Mayer and Fagundes, 2009), internal control (Ferrando and De La Parra, 2008), organizational culture (Domańska-Szaruga, 2020) or logistics (Tubis and Werbińska-Wojciechowska, 2021).

Table 1.1 Characteristic features of the existing risk management maturity models

Name of model	Author, year	Type	Application	Sector	Using
Hillson Risk Maturity Model	Hillson, 1997	Attributes	General management	All sectors	Self-assessment
Risk Exposure Calculator	Simons, 1999	Attributes with questionnaire	General management	All sectors	Self-assessment
Risk Management Maturity Level Development RMRP Version 1.0	Risk Management Research and Development Program Collaboration (RMRDPC), 2002	Attributes	Projects	All sectors	Self-assessment
IACCM Business Risk Management Maturity Model (BRM3)	International Association for Contract and Commercial Management (IACCM), 2003	Attributes with questionnaire	General management	All sectors	Self-assessment
Risk Management Capability Maturity Model for Complex Product Systems [CoPS] Projects	Ren and Yeo, 2004	Attributes with questionnaire	CoPS projects	CoPS providers	Self-assessment and respondents survey
	Yeo and Ren, 2009	Attributes with questionnaire	CoPS projects	CoPS providers in consumer goods and services	Self-assessment and respondents survey
HVR Project Risk Maturity Model	Hopkinson and Lovelock, 2004	Attributes with questionnaire	Projects	All sectors	Expert assessment
The Risk Management Process Maturity Model	Chapman, 2006	Attributes	General management	All sectors	Self-assessment

(continued)

Table 1.1 Cont.

Name of model	Author, year	Type	Application	Sector	Using
PMI's Risk Management Maturity Model	Loosemore et al., 2006	Attributes with questionnaire	Projects	All sectors	Self-assessment
RIMS Risk Maturity Model for Enterprise Risk Management	Risk and Insurance Management Society (RIMS), 2006	Attributes	General management	All sectors	Self-assessment
	Risk and Insurance Management Society (RIMS), 2015	Attributes with questionnaire	General management	All sectors	Self-assessment, respondents survey and expert assessment
Risk Management Capability Maturity Model	Macgillivray et al., 2007	Attributes	General management	Water utility sector	Self-assessment and external evaluation (voluntary or audit)
Capability Maturity Model for Information Risk Management	Lacey, 2007	Attributes	Information security management system	All sectors	Self-assessment
Operational Risk Management Maturity Model	Ferrando and De La Parra, 2008	Attributes with questionnaire	Internal control systems	Insurance	Self-assessment and respondents survey
Enterprise Risk Management Maturity – Level Assessment Tool	Ciorciari and Blattner, 2008	Attributes	General management	All sectors	Self-assessment

Model	Author, Year	Structure	Focus	Sector	Assessment method
ALARM National Performance Model for Risk Management in the Public Services	Public Risk Management Association ALARM, 2009	Attributes with questionnaire	General management	Public sector	Self-assessment and expert assessment
Model to Assess the Maturity Level of the Risk Management Process in Information Security MMGRSeg	Mayer and Fagundes, 2009	Attributes	Information security management system	All sectors	Self-assessment
Construction Risk Management Maturity Model	Öngel, 2009	Attributes with questionnaire	Projects	Construction	Self-assessment
Risk Management Maturity Model for Construction Organizations	Zou et al., 2010	Attributes with questionnaire	Projects	Construction	Self-assessment and external evaluation
Risk Maturity Index	AON & Wharton School of the University of Pennsylvania, 2011	Attributes with questionnaire	General management	All sectors	Respondents survey and expert assessment
Project Risk Maturity Model	Hopkinson, 2011	Attributes with questionnaire	Projects	All sectors	Respondents survey and expert assessment
Risk Maturity Model for Dutch municipalities	Cienfuegos Spikin, 2013	Attributes with questionnaire	General management	Public sector	Self-assessment and respondents survey
Overall Risk Management Maturity Level (ORMML)	Salawu and Abdullah, 2015	Attributes with questionnaire	Projects	Construction	Self-assessment and respondents survey

(continued)

Table 1.1 Cont.

Name of model	Author, year	Type	Application	Sector	Using
Risk Management Maturity Model	IIRM Investors in Risk Management, 2016	Attributes	General management	All sectors	Expert assessment
Maturity Model for Enterprise Risk Management (in supply chains)	Oliva, 2016	Attributes with questionnaire	General management	Supply chains	Respondents survey and expert assessment
Delloitte's Risk Maturity Model	Deloitte, 2016	Attributes	General management	All sectors	Self-assessment and expert assessment
Risk Management: A Maturity Model Based on ISO 31000	Proença et al., 2017	Attributes with questionnaire	General management	All sectors	Self-assessment and respondents survey
Generic Risk Maturity Model (GRMM) for evaluating risk management in construction projects	Hoseini et al., 2019	Attributes with questionnaire	Projects	Construction	Self-assessment and expert assessment
RM3 The Risk Management Maturity Model	Office of Rail and Road, 2019	Attributes	General management	Rail industry	Self-assessment and expert assessment
Model of Project Risk Management Maturity	Hartono et al., 2019	Attributes with questionnaire	Projects	Construction, ICT and telcoa industries	Self-assessment and respondents survey

Model	Author	Structure	Area	Application	Method
Risk Management Maturity Model for Automotive Industry	Čech and Januška, 2020	Attributes with questionnaire	General management	Automotive industry	Self-assessment, respondents survey and expert assessment
Maturity Model of Risk Management Culture	Domańska-Szaruga, 2020	Attributes with questionnaire	Organizational culture	Local government units	Respondents survey
Enterprise Risk Management Maturity Model	OECD, 2021	Attributes	General management	Tax administrations	Self-assessment
Risk Management Maturity Model for Logistic Processes	Tubis and Werbińska-Wojciechowska, 2021	Attributes	Logistics processes	Supply chains	Self-assessment and respondents survey

Source: the authors' own work.

Thus, in the second group, the models for assessing risk management maturity in the area of project management are the most numerous.

Using the criterion of a sector in which models could be applied, we found that most of the models under examination could be used without restrictions, i.e. in different types of organizations. Therefore, these models were being designed and developed to be universal. Nevertheless, there are models addressed to specific sectors, for example, the water utility sector (Macgillivray et al., 2007), insurance (Ferrando and De La Parra, 2008), public sector (ALARM, 2009; Cienfuegos Spikin, 2013), construction (Öngel, 2009; Zou et al., 2010; Salawu and Abdullah, 2015; Hoseini et al., 2019; Hartono et al., 2019), supply chains (Oliva, 2016; Tubis and Werbińska-Wojciechowska, 2021), rail industry (Office of Rail and Road, 2019), automotive industry (Čech and Januška, 2020), tax administrations (OECD, 2021) and local government units (Domańska-Szaruga, 2020). The sector-oriented models are intended for either private sectors or the public one.

The last criterion taken into account is the manner of using a model. A significant proportion of the models provide for an internal assessment formula in the form of an organization's self-assessment or self-assessment supported by respondents survey. In contrast, some models require the involvement of external experts (Hopkinson and Lovelock, 2004; RIMS, 2015; ALARM, 2009; AON & Wharton School of the University of Pennsylvania, 2011; Hopkinson, 2011; Oliva, 2016; Deloitte, 2016; Hoseini et al., 2019; Office of Rail and Road, 2019; Čech and Januška, 2020). Experts' opinions sometimes support self-assessment. There are also models in which assessment should be implemented as external evaluation – voluntary or audit (Macgillivray et al., 2007; Zou et al., 2010). Thus, we found that the models under comparison provided for three types of assessment: internal, external and mixed.

1.2.2 The attributes of risk management maturity assessment in the existing models

In the 34 models under examination, we identified a total of 45 attributes that undergo assessment (Table 1.2). They represent the following specific groups: improvement (I), cooperation (C), resources and competences (R), formalization (F), processes (P), social issues (S) and methodology (M).

In terms of frequency of occurrence, the attributes were divided into those occurring very frequently (in 20 or more models), those occurring with fairly high frequency (in 10–19 models) and those occurring less frequently (in fewer than 10 models). The very frequently occurring attributes are the following: Risk Management (RM) process, methods, techniques and tools (in 28 models) and organizational culture/internal environment (in 24 models). This means that the authors of the existing models of maturity assessment most often focused on the significance of tools to be used in risk management, as well as cultural determinants of maturity. In the latter case, they took into account the influence of an organization's culture and internal environment on the preventive and compensatory orientation in its activities. The set of the attributes occurring quite frequently in the models under analysis includes commitment/participating (in 15 models), monitoring, reporting and audits (in 14 models), information management and communication (in 13 models), competence/skills (in 13 models), experience (in 12 models), RM knowledge and technology (in 11 models), application/practice (in 10 models), management/governance (in 10 models), people, leadership and strategy and policies (in 10 models). The attributes listed above are diverse, covering issues related to the risk management function, available resources and competences, as well as the role of managers.

Analysing the maturity assessment attributes chronologically, we identified apparent trends and changes in their popularity over time. Initially (mainly in the years 1997–2004), the most commonly used attributes were those associated with a processual approach to risk and related to the competences, knowledge and experience of risk managers, as well as the communication and flow of information about risk and the methods of its management (cf. Hillson, 1997; Ren and Yeo, 2004).

The more recent models (those developed in the years 2006–2007) started to take into consideration a wider range of features, supplementing the existing attributes with new ones concerning, for example, the awareness of risks occurring in organizations, the organizational image, the integration of risk management into the overall organizational management system, or the integration of the human factor into risk management, including the role of leadership or the degree of decentralization of planning and risk management tasks (cf. Loosemore et al., 2006; Lacey, 2007).

Subsequently, from 2007 onwards, selecting attributes for assessment models, their authors started to take into account the need to formalize the risk management process, for example, in terms of building a risk management strategy and/or policy, implementing standards and procedures, as well as developing organizational learning and continuous improvement functions, mainly through monitoring, reporting and control (cf. Macgillivray et al., 2007; Deloitte, 2016; Hartono et al., 2019).

Table 1.2 Attributes assessed in the existing risk management maturity models

Model	F	S	M	R	I	I	P	R
	Definition / context	Organizational culture / Internal environment	RM process, methods, techniques and tools	Experience	Application / Practice	Growth	Information management and communication	RM knowledge and technology
Hillson, 1997	✓	✓	✓	✓	✓			
Simons, 1999		✓				✓	✓	
RMRDPC, 2002		✓	✓	✓	✓			
IACCM, 2003		✓	✓	✓	✓			
Ren and Yeo 2004		✓	✓	✓				✓
Yeo and Ren 2009		✓	✓	✓				✓
Hopkinson and Lovelock, 2004		✓	✓					
Chapman, 2006		✓			✓			
Loosemore et al., 2006		✓	✓	✓	✓			
RIMS, 2006								
RIMS, 2015								
Macgillivray et al., 2007								
Lacey, 2007							✓	✓
Ferrando and De La Parra, 2008		✓	✓	✓				
Ciorciari and Blattner, 2008		✓	✓				✓	
ALARM, 2009			✓					
Mayer and Fagundes, 2009	✓	✓					✓	
Öngel, 2009		✓	✓	✓	✓			
Zou et al., 2010		✓	✓		✓			
AON & Wharton School, 2011		✓	✓				✓	
Hopkinson, 2011		✓	✓					
Cienfuegos Spikin, 2013	✓	✓						
Salawu and Abdullah, 2015		✓	✓	✓	✓			✓
IIRM, 2016	✓	✓	✓				✓	
Oliva, 2016			✓				✓	✓
Deloitte, 2016		✓	✓					✓
Proença et al., 2017	✓		✓				✓	
Hoseini et al., 2019		✓	✓		✓			✓
Office of Rail and Road, 2019		✓	✓				✓	✓
Hartono et al., 2019		✓	✓	✓	✓		✓	✓
Čech and Januška, 2020		✓	✓		✓		✓	✓
Domańska-Szaruga, 2020	✓	✓	✓				✓	
OECD, 2021		✓	✓				✓	
Tubis and Werbińska-Wojciechowska, 2021			✓	✓				✓
Total	6	24	28	12	10	1	13	11

R	C	P	F	R	P	I	S	S	R	M	P	P	M	M	P	I
Competence / Skills	Stakeholders relationships and partnership	Project management	System	Training	Management / Governance	Awareness	Image	Trust / Confidence	Resources	Adoption of ERM-based approach	ERM process management	Risk appetite management	Root cause discipline	Uncovering risks / Visibility of incidents	Performance management	Business resiliency and sustainability
✓	✓															
✓	✓															
	✓	✓														
			✓	✓	✓											
✓						✓	✓	✓	✓							
										✓	✓	✓	✓	✓	✓	✓
										✓	✓	✓	✓	✓	✓	✓
✓	✓								✓							
✓	✓													✓		
✓														✓		
	✓				✓				✓							
✓						✓	✓	✓	✓							
					✓											
✓					✓											
		✓	✓													
✓						✓		✓	✓							
			✓													
					✓											
	✓				✓	✓			✓			✓				
	✓			✓	✓				✓							
✓																
✓	✓		✓		✓											
✓				✓		✓										
✓					✓			✓	✓			✓				
			✓			✓								✓	✓	
					✓											
13	9	2	5	3	10	6	2	4	8	2	2	4	2	5	3	2

Table 1.2 Cont.

Model	Attributes					
	F	P	I	I	I	F
	Scope	Integration with other processes	Verification and validation	Reviewing, feedback and organizational learning	Monitoring, reporting and audits	Documentation, procedures and standards
Hillson, 1997						
Simons, 1999						
RMRDPC, 2002						
IACCM, 2003						
Ren and Yeo 2004		✓				
Yeo and Ren 2009		✓				
Hopkinson and Lovelock, 2004						
Chapman, 2006						
Loosemore et al., 2006						
RIMS, 2006						
RIMS, 2015						
Macgillivray et al., 2007	✓	✓	✓	✓	✓	✓
Lacey, 2007						✓
Ferrando and De La Parra, 2008						
Ciorciari and Blattner, 2008					✓	
ALARM, 2009						
Mayer and Fagundes, 2009					✓	
Öngel, 2009						
Zou et al., 2010						✓
AON & Wharton School, 2011						
Hopkinson, 2011						
Cienfuegos Spikin, 2013				✓		
Salawu and Abdullah, 2015	✓			✓	✓	✓
IIRM, 2016				✓	✓	
Oliva, 2016					✓	
Deloitte, 2016					✓	
Proença et al., 2017				✓	✓	
Hoseini et al., 2019				✓	✓	
Office of Rail and Road, 2019				✓	✓	✓
Hartono et al., 2019		✓				✓
Čech and Januška, 2020	✓	✓		✓	✓	✓
Domańska-Szaruga, 2020		✓			✓	✓
OECD, 2021				✓	✓	
Tubis and Werbińska-Wojciechowska, 2021					✓	
Total	3	6	1	9	14	8

Source: the authors' own work.

I	R	F	I	F	P	C	C	F	I	I	P	P	C
Practical effects / Outcomes evaluation	People, leadership and commitment / participating	Strategy and policies	Benchmarking of costs / benefits	Objective setting	Decision making	External support	External disclosure	Ownership of risks	Improvements	Management of assets	Change management	Attitude towards risk / risk management	Cooperation at risk
					✓								
	✓											✓	
	✓											✓	
	✓	✓	✓										
✓													
	✓	✓		✓									
✓	✓	✓											
	✓												
	✓	✓			✓								
				✓	✓								
	✓											✓	
	✓					✓							
		✓			✓		✓	✓					
✓	✓		✓	✓				✓	✓				
	✓	✓							✓				
	✓	✓		✓									
✓	✓	✓											
	✓		✓							✓	✓	✓	
	✓	✓							✓		✓		
		✓											
													✓
4	15	10	3	4	4	1	1	2	3	1	2	4	1

Thus, we noticed, on the one hand, the emergence of new attributes in the successive maturity assessment models and, on the other hand, the inclusiveness of the models consisting in the fact that some attributes were included throughout the development of the maturity models (e.g. RM process, methods, techniques and tools or organizational culture/internal environment) and were successively complemented by newly created attributes. This indicates the evolutionary nature of the development of risk management maturity assessment models over the 25 years covered by our analysis.

1.2.3 The scales of risk management maturity assessment in the existing models

In our analysis of the existing RMMM, we also paid particular attention to their assessment scales (Table 1.3).

In most of the analysed models, a five-grade scale is used to assess the maturity of risk management. In a few of them, the scale starts from level 0, which indicates that risk management does not function at all in a given organization (RIMS 2006; 2015; Proença et al., 2017) or that its approach to this issue is reactive (Čech and Januška, 2020). However, the majority of the scales start from level 1, which signifies the presence of a certain, as yet unspecified and unformalized approach to risk in an organization. Actions resulting from this approach are taken without much preparation, on an ad hoc basis. This level of maturity is most often referred to as initial (in 9 models), ad hoc (in 8 models) or naive (in 4 models). Different terms are used to describe intermediate levels of maturity, indicate the progressing evolution of the risk management process, highlight the cyclical character and recurrence of actions taken to address risks or emphasize the formalization and integration of such actions and their effectiveness. The expressions used to define the highest level of maturity indicate professionalization, sophistication of activities and achievement of excellence. We also identified models whose scales for assessing risk management maturity deviated from those dominating in the other models. In two models (Hoseini et al., 2019; Hartono et al., 2019), there are no defined maturity levels. Instead, assessment is performed by means of a numerical scoring system using a maturity score.

Table 1.3 The assessment scales adopted in the existing risk management maturity models

Model	Maturity levels					
	0	1	2	3	4	5
Hillson, 1997		Naive	Novice	Normalized	Natural	
Simons, 1999		Safety Zone	Caution Zone	Danger Zone		
RMRDPC, 2002		Ad hoc	Initial	Repeatable	Managed	
IACCM, 2003		Novice	Competent	Proficient	Expert	
Ren and Yeo 2004		Initial	Repeatable	Defined	Managed	Optimized
Yeo and Ren 2009		Initial	Repeatable	Defined	Managed	Optimized
Hopkinson & Lovelock, 2004		Naive	Novice	Normalized	Natural	
Chapman, 2006		Initial	Basic	Standard	Advanced	
Loosemore et al., 2006		Ad hoc	Defined	Managed	Integrated	
RIMS, 2006	Non existent	Ad hoc	Initial	Repeatable	Managed	Leadership
RIMS, 2015	Non existent	Ad hoc	Initial	Repeatable	Managed	Leadership
Macgillivray et al., 2007		Initial	Repeatable	Defined	Controlled	Optimized
Lacey, 2007		Informal and ad hoc	Planned and tracked	Defined and institutionalized	Managed and measured	Optimized and agile
Ferrando and De La Parra, 2008		Traditional	Awareness	Monitoring	Quantification	Integration
Ciorciari and Blattner, 2008		Very weak	Poor	Middle	Good	Optimized
ALARM, 2009		Engaging	Happening	Working	Embedded	Driving
Mayer and Fagundes, 2009		Initial	Known	Standardized	Managed	Optimized
Öngel, 2009		Ad hoc	Established	Managed	Integrated	
Zou et al., 2010		Initial and ad hoc	Repeatable	Managed	Optimized	
AON & Wharton School, 2011		Initial	Basic	Defined	Operational	Advanced
Hopkinson, 2011		Naive	Novice	Normalized	Natural	
Cienfuegos Spikin, 2013		Initial	Repeatable	Defined	Managed	Optimized
Salawu and Abdullah, 2015		Naive	Novice	Managed	Optimized	Optimized

(continued)

Table 1.3 Cont.

Model	Maturity levels					
	0	*1*	*2*	*3*	*4*	*5*
IIRM, 2016		Very basic	Basic	Emerging	Mature	Advanced
Oliva, 2016		Insufficient	Contingency	Structured	Participative	Risk Intelligent
Deloitte, 2016		Initial	Fragmented	Top down	Integrated	Optimizing
Proença et al., 2017	Non existent	Initial	Managed	Defined	Quantitatively Managed	
Hoseini et al., 2019	No maturity levels – instead scoring system (maturity score 1–10)					
Office of Rail and Road, 2019		Ad hoc	Managed	Standardized	Predictable	Excellence
Hartono et al., 2019	No maturity levels – instead scoring system (maturity score 1.2–2.7)					
Čech and Januška, 2020	Reactive	Aware	Proactive	Adult	Risk-smart	
Domańska-Szaruga, 2020		Reactive	Institutional	Effective	Optimal	
OECD, 2021		Emerging	Progressing	Established	Leading	Aspirational
Tubis and Werbińska-Wojciechowska, 2021		Poor	Basic	Good	Satisfactory	Excellent

Source: the authors' own work.

References

Antonucci, D. (2016). *Risk Maturity Models – How to Assess Risk Management Effectiveness.* London: Kogan Page Limited.

AON & Wharton School of the University of Pennsylvania (2011). Risk Maturity Index, www.aon.com/risk-maturity-index (Access: 25.11.2021).

Aven, T. (2016). Risk assessment and risk management: Review of recent advances on their foundation. *European Journal of Operational Research,* 253(1), pp. 1–13.

Caiadoa, R.G.G., Limaa, G.B.A., de Mattos Nascimentoa, D.L., Netoa, J.V., Maultasch de Oliveiraa, R.A. (2016). Guidelines to risk management maturity in construction projects. *Brazilian Journal of Operations & Production Management,* 13, pp. 372–385.

Čech, M., Januška, M. (2020). Evaluation of risk management maturity in the Czech automotive industry: Model and methodology. *Amfiteatru Economic,* 55, pp. 824–845.

Chapman, R.J. (2006). *Simple Tools and Techniques for Enterprise Risk Management.* 2nd Edition. New York: Wiley Finance Series.

Chapman, R.J. (2011). *Simple Tools and Techniques for Enterprise Risk Management.* New York: John Wiley & Sons Ltd.

Cienfuegos Spikin, I.J. (2013). Developing a Risk Management Maturity Model: A Comprehensive Risk Maturity Model for Dutch Municipalities. Dissertation, Universiteit Twente.

Ciorciari, M., Blattner, P. (2008). Enterprise Risk Management Maturity-Level Assessment Tool. ERM Symposium, Chicago. www.soa.org/globalassets/ass ets/files/resources/essays-monographs/2008-erm-symposium/mono-2008-m-as08-1-ciorciari-abstract.pdf (Access: 25.11.2021).

de Bruin, T., Kulkarni, U., Freeze, R.D., Rosemann, M. (2005). Understanding the Main Phases of Developing a Maturity Assessment Model. Australasian (ACIS) 2005 Proceedings, 16th Australasian Conference on Information Systems, Sydney, Australia, 29 Nov–2 Dec 2005.

Deloitte (2016). Delloitte's Risk Maturity Model, www2.deloitte.com/content/ dam/Deloitte/uk/Documents/audit/deloitte-uk-erm-a-risk-intelligent-appro ach.pdf (Access: 25.11.2021).

Domańska-Szaruga, B. (2020). Maturity of risk management culture. *Entrepreneurship and Sustainability Issues* 7(3), pp. 2060–2078.

Ferrando, A., De La Parra, C. (2008). Operational risk management maturity model. BDO Audiberia. Congreso Iberico de Actuarioslisboa Mayo 2008.

Fisher, D.M. (2004). The business process maturity model. A practical approach for identifying opportunities for optimization. *Business Process Trends,* 9(4), 11–15.

Haffer, R. (2011). *Samoocena i pomiar wyników działalności w systemach zarządzania przedsiębiorstw: w poszukiwaniu doskonałości biznesowej.* Toruń: Wydawnictwo Naukowe Mikołaja Kopernika.

Harmon, P. (2004). Evaluating an organization's business process maturity. *Business Process Trends,* 2(3), 1–11.

Hartono, B., Wijaya, D.F., Arini, H.M. (2019). The impact of project risk management maturity on performance: Complexity as a moderating variable. *International Journal of Engineering Business Management*, 11, pp. 1–16.

Hillson, D. (1997). Toward a risk maturity model. *International Journal of Project & Business Risk Management*, 1(1), pp. 35–45.

Hopkinson, M. (2011). *The Project Risk Maturity Model: Measuring and Improving Risk Management Capability*. Farnham, UK: Gower Publishing, Ltd.

Hopkinson, M., Lovelock, G. (2004). The project risk maturity model – assessment of the U.K. MoD's top 30 acquisition projects. Paper presented at PMI® Global Congress 2004 – EMEA, Prague, Czech Republic. Newtown Square, PA: Project Management Institute.

Hoseini, E., Hertogh, M., Bosch-Rekveldt, M. (2019). Developing a generic risk maturity model (GRMM) for evaluating risk management in construction projects. *Journal of Risk Research*, 24(7), pp. 889–908.

IIRM Investors in Risk Management (2016). Risk Management Maturity Model, www.iirmglobal.com/risk-maturity-assessment/risk-management-maturity-model (Access: 25.11.2021).

International Association for Contract and Commercial Management (IACCM) (2003). Organisational Maturity in Business Risk Management: The IACCM Business Risk Management Maturity Model (BRM3), www.worldcc.com/Resources/Content-Hub/View/ArticleId/4737/The-IACCM-Business-Risk-Management-Maturity-Model-BRM3 (Access: 25.11.2021).

Jedynak, P., Bąk, S. (2018). Modele oceny dojrzałości zarządzania ryzykiem. *Problemy Jakości*, 50(10), pp. 12–18.

Kania, K. (2013). *Doskonalenie zarządzania procesami biznesowymi w organizacji z wykorzystaniem modeli dojrzałości i technologii informacyjno-komunikacyjnych*. Katowice: Wydawnictwo Uniwersytetu Ekonomicznego w Katowicach.

Kwak, Y.H., Ibbs, C.W. (2002). Project management process maturity (PM) 2 model. *Journal of Management in Engineering*, 18, pp. 150–155.

Lacey, D. (2007). A capability maturity model for information risk management. White Paper by Chronicle Solutions. www.chroniclesolutions.com/.

Loosemore, M., Raftery, J., Reilly, C., Higgon, D. (2006). *Risk Management in Projects*. London: Taylor & Francis.

Macgillivray, B.H., Sharp J.V, Strutt, J.E., Hamilton, P.D., Pollard, S.J.T. (2007). Benchmarking risk management within the international water utility sector. Part I: Design of a capability maturity methodology. *Journal of Risk Research*, 10(1), pp. 85–104.

Mayer, J., Fagundes, L.L. (2009). A Model to Assess the Maturity Level of the Risk Management Process in Information Security. Integrated Network Management-Workshops. IM'09. IFIP/IEEE International Symposium.

OECD (2021). Enterprise Risk Management Maturity Model, www.oecd.org/tax/forum-on-tax-administration/publications-and-products/enterprise-risk-management-maturity-model.pdf (Access: 23.11.2021).

Office of Rail and Road (2019). RM3 The Risk Management Maturity Model, https://iosh.com/media/5351/risk-management-maturity-model.pdf (Access: 24.11.2021).

Oliva, F.L. (2016). A maturity model for enterprise risk management. *International Journal of Production Economics*, 173(C), pp. 66–79.

Öngel, B. (2009). Assessing Risk Management Maturity: A Framework for the Construction Companies. Dumlupinar Bulvari (1). https://etd.lib.metu.edu.tr/upload/12611457/index.pdf (Access: 25.11.2021).

Pöppelbuß, J., Roglinger, M. (2011). What makes a useful maturity model? A framework of general design principles for maturity models and its demonstration in Business Process Management. ECIS 2011 Proceedings Paper 28. http://aisel.aisnet.org/ecis2011/28 (Access: 25.11.2021).

Proença, D., Vieira, R., Estevens, J., Borbinha, J. (2017). Risk Management: A Maturity Model Based on ISO 31000. IEEE 19th Conference on Business Informatics (CBI), pp. 99–108. doi:10.1109/CBI.2017.40. www.researchgate.net/publication/319218604_Risk_Management_A_Maturity_Model_Based_on_ISO_31000 (Access: 26.11.2021).

Public Risk Management Association ALARM (2009). ALARM National Performance Model for Risk Management in the Public Services, www.london.gov.uk/about-us/londonassembly/meetings/documents/s40227/07%20-%20Appendix%203%20-%20Alarm%20National%20Performance%20Model%202.pdf (Access: 24.11.2021).

Ren, Y., Yeo K.T. (2004). Risk Management Capability Maturity Model for Complex Product Systems (CoPS) Projects. International Engineering Management Conference, Singapore.

RIMS (Risk and Insurance Management Society) (2006). Risk Maturity Model (RMM) for Enterprise Risk Management, www.logicmanager.com/pdf/rims_rmm_executive_summary.pdf (Access: 22.11.2021).

RIMS (Risk and Insurance Management Society) (2015). Risk Maturity Model for Enterprise Risk Management, www.riskmaturitymodel.org/risk-maturity-model-rmm-for-erm/ (Access: 22.11.2021).

Risk Management Research and Development Program Collaboration (RMRDPC) (2002). Risk Management Maturity Level Development RMRP Version 1.0. Formal Collaboration: INCOSE Risk Management Working Group, Project Management Institute Risk Management Specific Interest Group, UK Association for Project Management, Risk Specific Interest Group.

Salawu, R.A., Abdullah, F. (2015). Assessing risk management maturity of construction organisations on infrastructural project delivery in Nigeria. *Procedia – Social and Behavioral Sciences*, 172(27), pp. 643–650.

Saleh, M. (2011). Information security maturity model. *International Journal of Computer Science and Security*, 5(3), pp. 316–337.

Schiller, F., Prpich, G. (2014). Learning to organise risk management in organisations: What future for enterprise risk management? *Journal of Risk Research*, 17(8), pp. 999–1017.

Simons, R. (1999). How risky is your company? *Harvard Business Review*, 77(3), pp. 85–94.

Tubis, A.A., Werbińska-Wojciechowska, S. (2021). Risk management maturity model for logistic processes. *Sustainability*, 13(2), p. 659.

Wieczorek-Kosmala, M. (2014). Risk management practices from risk maturity models. *Journal for East European Management Studies*, 19(2), pp. 133–159.

Yeo, K.T., Ren, Y. (2009). Risk management capability maturity model for complex product systems (CoPS) projects. *Systems Engineering*, 12(4), pp. 275–294.

Zou, P.X.W., Chen, Y., Chan, T-Y. (2010). Understanding and improving your risk management capability: Assessment model for construction organizations. *Journal of Construction Engineering and Management*, 136(8), pp. 854–863.

2 Crisis situations and risk management maturity

2.1 Crisis in enterprise management

A crisis in an enterprise's operations is most often equated with an unexpected, potentially disruptive situation that can threaten its objectives as well as impact its internal environment and external relationships (Coombs and Holladay, 2002; Bundy et al., 2017). Crisis can also present an opportunity for business improvement, but only if decision makers take advantage of it properly (Brockner and James, 2008). Furthermore, crisis is most often a dynamic process that is usually not limited to triggering changes in one area, but tends to spread throughout an enterprise and beyond (Hart et al., 2001). Crisis situations follow either continuous or sudden changes in the business environment. Such changes force enterprises to tackle increasingly difficult adaptation demands which, if not met, can threaten the continuity of business operations (Mikušová and Horváthová, 2019).

Crisis experienced by an enterprise is in each case a specific management situation which very often requires the development of adaptation mechanisms or the implementation of corrective and remedial actions neutralizing to the highest possible extent the scale of negative consequences resulting from a crisis situation (Jedynak and Bąk, 2021). Adopted by an enterprise's management team, a specific way of proceeding in crisis depends on the type of difficulties they experience.

The most general classification divides crises into external and internal. External crises have their sources outside an enterprise and often affect either whole sectors or all enterprises, having a macroeconomic character. Internal crises affecting a business organization may originate in various areas of its activity such as management processes, sales, production, logistics, customer relations, investments, finance, development, etc. The sources of such crises include, for example (Zelek, 2003), mistakes in management, inadequate financial control, high level

DOI: 10.4324/9781003330905-3

of costs, marketing mistakes, lack or weakening of competitive advantage, overinvestment and weakening financial condition.

The main types of management crises distinguished on the basis of various criteria are presented in Table 2.1.

Crises generate a number of implications of organizational, personnel, financial, technological, procedural, logistical, reputational, etc., nature. The catalogue of challenges faced by managers during a crisis situation includes the following: (1) quickly integrating information and designing decision-making processes based on it in hitherto unknown circumstances (Thürmer et al., 2020), (2) revising the existing corporate management strategy and coordinating it with the changes that need to be implemented in response to a crisis (Bayazıt et al., 2003; Wenzel et al., 2020), (3) developing an appropriate crisis management strategy adapted to the internal and external environment of an organization (Litovchenko, 2012), (4) applying the rules of crisis leadership (Wang and Belardo, 2005; Karim, 2016), (5) skilfully delegating powers and responsibilities in the crisis management process (Cener, 2007), (6) reorganizing key processes (Slatter and Lovett, 2001), (7) developing crisis adaptation measures and using post-crisis changes for the further growth of an enterprise (Mikušová and Horváthová, 2019).

The wider the range of problems emerging with a crisis, the more important is the dynamics of managers' responses to them. If an escalating crisis is not contained and properly managed in due time, it may trigger a chain reaction of problems occurring and spreading rapidly problems within an enterprise and even among its stakeholders (Fener and Cevik, 2015). A particular threat to an enterprise is such an escalation of a crisis that results in the transformation of a difficult situation into a crisis of a strategic nature. A strategic crisis is characterized by a malfunctioning of basic business mechanisms, a sharp slowdown or stoppage in an enterprise's development, abrupt inhibition or prevention of further development and the management system's loss of the ability to self-regulate (Shiller, 2012, Groh, 2014).

2.2 The COVID-19 pandemic as a specific type of crisis

The COVID-19 pandemic is a source of unique types of crisis that have been experienced with various intensity by enterprises from many different sectors since the beginning of 2020. Similarly, it has not been a neutral force for business management systems. Both enterprises negatively affected by the consequences of the pandemic and those for whom they have been a source of growth and improved competitive position (Jedynak and Bąk, 2021) have been forced to adapt their management

Table 2.1 The types of crises in enterprise management

Criterion of distinction	Type of crisis	Crisis characteristics
Source of crisis	Economic crisis	Market crisis, financial crisis, growth crisis, crisis resulting from legal changes, employment crisis
	Information crisis	Communication problems, problems with access to market information, loss of data or failure to keep data or information confidential
	Physical crisis	Production disruptions, problems with quality of products/services
	Human resources crisis	Loss of employees, employee frauds
	Image-related crisis	Negative opinions
	Crisis related to natural disasters and terrorism	Related to natural disasters and terrorism
Adaptability	Crisis of adaptation	It manifests itself in problems with adaptation to threats; the most common cause is the petrification of organizational structures and management procedures
	Crisis of continuity	It consists in a lack of inertia, is caused by disruptions of the management process due to constant changes.
Processual character	Potential crisis	A threat to an enterprise's activities and pursuit of objectives resulting from the negative influence of various external and internal phenomena
	Hidden crisis	Difficulties in achieving an enterprise's objectives and managing its resources, often equated with so-called transitional difficulties
	Overt crisis	Appearance of difficulties in the functioning of an enterprise whose consequences may threaten its economic existence
Life cycle	Leadership crisis	Growth of an enterprise to such an extent that it exceeds the controlling abilities of its founder or initiator – it usually results in a loss of control over the enterprise's growing range of operations and size
	Crisis of autonomy	Appearance of chaos in the established organizational structure, loss of control over supervised areas of an enterprise's activities at the particular hierarchical levels
	Crisis of decentralization	It forces managers to focus on better coordination of decentralized activities and may indicate the beginning of another phase of an enterprise's growth

(continued)

Table 2.1 Cont.

Criterion of distinction	Type of crisis	Crisis characteristics
	Crisis of bureaucratization	Decrease of the effectiveness of functioning of large enterprises due to their natural tendency to expand bureaucracy and thus increase fixed costs
	Crisis of maturity	It is connected with an enterprise's failure to continue its development
Time	Sudden crisis	Disturbances in conducting business activities that appear without warning
	Smouldering crisis	Each business problem growing in time, regardless of its source
Nature of crisis	Internal crisis	It constitutes a subsystem of management, is caused by factors occurring within an enterprise, such as improper management or a wrong financial policy
	External crisis	Its causes are mainly macroeconomic processes, new social phenomena, technological progress, market globalization, etc.
Pace of crisis	Sudden/immediate crisis	It is characterized by a lack of time for research and planning, decisions have to be taken immediately
	Chronic crisis	It may last for months or even years, a long period of time is not conducive to taking effective measures to contain a crisis
Reality of crisis	Real crisis	It is caused by various factors and usually leads to many problems in an enterprise
	Virtual crisis	It is artificially created in order to bring about changes and, consequently, develop and increase an enterprise's revenue base
Course of crisis	Type I crisis	It is characterized by a gradual intensification of negative effects and a long-lasting accumulation of crisis phenomena
	Type II crisis	It is characterized by a medium duration, rapid spreading and variable intensity of destructive effects
	Type III crisis	Is characterised by a short duration, rapid course and very fast accumulation of destructive effects

Source: the authors' own work based on: Krystek (1987); Mitroff (2004); Sienkiewicz-Małyjurek (2015); Zelek (2003); Ziarko and Walas-Trębacz (2010).

processes to significantly different conditions of conducting business activities (Li et al., 2021). The identification, analysis and assessment of the risks caused by COVID-19 were hampered by the intensity, dynamism and unpredictability of the social and economic changes generated by the pandemic. The hallmark of these risks is the difficulty of applying preventive measures and, consequently, the impossibility of implementing any preventive strategy (Jedynak and Bąk, 2021).

From the perspective of business management, the COVID-19 pandemic has generated a number of circumstances constituting the consequences of the emergence of various financial, organizational, strategic, as well as global risk factors (Jedynak and Bąk, 2021). As regards financial problems, business managers face the challenge of dealing with, among others, the following problems: liquidity (Maurin et al., 2020; Bircan et al., 2020), insurability of risks (Richter and Wilson, 2020), pricing (Abdelnour et al., 2020) or creditworthiness (Koulouridi et al., 2020). On the other hand, in the case of organizational issues, the COVID-19 pandemic has forced business organizations to take specific actions in response to formal and legal problems related to pandemic restrictions (Ernst & Young, 2020) and staffing issues (Gartner, 2020). Another area of managerial challenges during the pandemic comprises strategic problems, mainly concerning maintaining business continuity under new conditions (Gourinchas et al., 2020), counteracting reputational loss, e.g. through development in the CSR area (He and Harris, 2020), or adjusting investment processes, mainly in terms of foreign investment (Unctad, 2020). The main sources of challenges for corporate management in the category of global problems are complications with cooperation within global supply chains (Craven et al., 2020; Hedwall, 2020) and technological problems (Splett, 2020).

For enterprises, the phenomena resulting from the COVID-19 pandemic are either a significant source of problems in various areas of activity or an opportunity for growth and improved performance. The determinants of failure or success of business organizations during the COVID-19 pandemic, are presented in Table 2.2.

In response to the effects of the COVID-19 pandemic on enterprises, managers have faced the challenge of implementing dynamic and resolute measures to maintain business continuity (in the case of companies negatively affected by the pandemic) or exploiting growth opportunities created by the pandemic phenomena (in the case of companies experiencing positive consequences of the pandemic).

In the case of companies experiencing the negative consequences of the pandemic crisis, the actions of management teams should be directed mainly at mitigating the identified threats and fighting their

Table 2.2 The determinants of failure or success of enterprises during the COVID-19 pandemic

Determinants of success	Determinants of failure
(1) Strategy: — Business continuity plan — Continuous risk assessment — Strategic partnership — Coopetition — Investment — Scenarios — Community involvement — Diversification	(1) Law and economy: — Reduction of activity — Pandemic in enterprises — Fee collection prohibition — Lack of aid — Health restrictions — Fall in interest rates
(2) Business model: — Digitalization — Fractionalization — Scale of operations — Production/service capacity — Operational efficiency — Supply chain effectiveness — Price competitiveness	(2) Sector: — Fall in prices and margins — Destabilization of demand — Global drop in supply — Logistic problems
	(3) Customers: — Customers' problems — Changes in purchasing behaviours — Changes in working methods — Long-term contracts — Necessity of concessions — Poor customer structure
(3) Resources: — Initial capital — Relational capital — Trust of partners — Owner — Experience — Strong R&D — Logistic infrastructure — Employee competences — Growth potential	(4) Finance: — Bad initial situation — Lack of financial reserves — Debt-based strategy — Additional costs — High fixed costs — Problems with rapid re-education of costs
(4) Flexibility: — Monitoring the environment — Rapid response — Rapid implementation of innovations — Finding financing sources — Structural changes — Legal adaptability	(5) Resources: — Large permanent staff — Excess of tangible investments — Large stocks
(5) Services/products: — Market quality — Service quality — Comprehensiveness of services — Multiplication of innovations — Versatility of services — Delivery time	(6) Management: — Strategy mismatch — Poor forecasting — Slowness in decision-making — Overestimation of survival possibilities — Naivety — Lack of product diversification — Lack of location diversification

Table 2.2 Cont.

Determinants of success	Determinants of failure
(6) Customer relations: — Loyalty programmes — Dynamic marketing — Customer communication — Social media	(7) Sales: — Dominance of stationary sales — Low digitalization of sales — Limitations of digital sales — Slow digital transformation
(7) Environment: — Macroeconomic situation — Increase in demand — Changes in customer preferences — Technological megatrends	

Source: the authors' own work based on: Jedynak and Bąk (2021).

own weaknesses in the following areas (Jedynak and Bąk, 2021): (1) reducing the negative impact of the macro-environment, (2) reducing sectoral risks, (3) responding adequately to troubles in customer relations, (4) preventing financial problems, (5) taking care of resources, (6) reducing managerial deficiencies and (7) improving the sales strategy.

On the other hand, for enterprises that can use the experience of the pandemic crisis to improve their position, management actions should be mainly focused on exploiting opportunities and developing strengths, especially those related to (Jedynak and Bąk, 2021): (1) exploring the strategic fit, (2) exploiting business model strengths, (3) leveraging resource potential, (4) discounting flexibility, (5) competing based on products and services, (6) leveraging customer relationships and (7) taking advantage of positive changes in the environment.

2.3 Challenges to risk management in crisis

On the one hand, a crisis in an enterprise can be (and most often is) the cause of many problems in its activities; on the other hand, it can be a stimulator of development and improvement of the competitive position. Therefore, the adopted principles and methods of management during a crisis may determine its final consequences for an enterprise. Of course, the external conditions of a crisis are often independent of the adopted crisis management strategy; nevertheless, a right crisis strategy can significantly mitigate the negative effects of a crisis (Jedynak and Bąk, 2021). This is why crisis management has an indisputable role in determining the ultimate degree of severity of a crisis situation for an enterprise.

In the most general terms, crisis management is a process by which a company takes adequate measures to deal with a disruptive and unexpected event that threatens to harm both the company, its stakeholders and society at large (Bundy et al., 2017). Crisis management can thus be described as the coordination of complex systems and the design of an organizational structure in such a way that the process serves to prevent crisis situations, reduce the scale and scope of their negative consequences, as well as improve based on the lessons learned from past crises (Bigley and Roberts, 2001; Gephart et al., 2009; Pearson and Clair, 1998; Starbuck and Milliken, 1988). Therefore, the process of crisis management goes significantly beyond a list of planned crisis prevention measures to include communication, which has three primary objectives. The first is an objective formulated even before a crisis occurs and concerns minimizing the likelihood of its occurrence. The second objective is formulated already during the course of a crisis and focuses mainly on minimizing its scale and scope of potential damage. The third objective is crucial already after a crisis and focuses on restoring the normal functioning of an enterprise (Bundy and Pfarrer, 2015; Kahn et. al., 2013; Pearson and Clair, 1998).

The crisis management process itself is holistic and can be divided into the following phases (Jaques, 2007; Coombs and Hollady, 2002): (1) the preparation (pre-crisis) phase, which includes forecasting, risk estimation, preventive measures and preparation for a possible crisis, (2) the decision-making phase, which includes responses to crisis events and (3) the post-crisis phase, which includes mitigation of the negative effects of a crisis, restoration of normal functioning, verification of implemented anti-crisis strategies and improvement actions.

When one takes into account that the core of crisis management is the integration of prevention and counteraction (Glaesser, 2006), what becomes evident is the special role that risk management plays in managing an enterprise during crisis.

Indeed, crisis management and risk management are undoubtedly closely related management domains. It is not uncommon to see the former contained within the latter (Shayb, 2017; Ndlela, 2018; Jedynak and Bąk, 2021). In essence, crisis management is an important component of a risk management system, representing a holistic approach to the risks faced by business organizations. Risk management and crisis management should therefore function on a feedback basis. It should also be borne in mind that crisis management cannot be limited to anti-crisis measures only. One of its objectives should also be to anticipate the future in order to prevent crises or to prepare enterprises for their possible occurrence. Moreover, as one of the main management domains, crisis management cannot be limited to episodic activities, either. It should be a continuous process, permanently embedded in the enterprise management system, compatible with risk management at the prevention stage and with business continuity management at the counteracting stage (Jedynak and Bąk, 2021).

On the other hand, despite the fact that risk management is commonly considered to be a process of mainly preventive nature (Ndlela, 2018), aiming to minimize the possibility of negative events occurring to the maximum extent (which represents the best way to anticipate and prevent crises), one of its implicit objectives is also to minimize the scale of negative consequences of such events. Thus, risk management processes, and especially the phases of risk identification, analysis and assessment, may prove to be effective tools for streamlining management and improving its efficiency once a crisis has actually occurred. In such circumstances, management does not address the risk of a potential crisis, but takes the form of measures targeted at the risk of negative consequences. Risk management during a crisis can also contribute to limiting the scale of such consequences. A crisis in the activities of an enterprise can undoubtedly be a source of both opportunities and threats, so risk management in a crisis situation has two key objectives: (1) to support the success factors in enterprises for which a crisis becomes a stimulus to exploit previously unknown opportunities and (2) to limit the failure factors in enterprises for which a crisis is a source of serious threats that should be eliminated as much as possible in order to maintain the continuity of operations (Jedynak and Bąk, 2021).

2.4 The maturity of risk management in crisis situations

Measuring the maturity of an enterprise's risk management can have positive results in many areas of its operation. The awareness of the degree of professionalization, scope and effectiveness of risk management processes carried out within an enterprise can significantly assist management teams in, on the one hand, making a credible assessment of the risk management system in place and, on the other hand, allowing for the identification of imperfections and designing improvement measures in the face of exposed weaknesses of the system.

It is recommended that specific aspects determining the level of risk management maturity be measured, which include, among others: organizational culture, risk management processes, business experience, organizational structure, sector, company size, performance and market value, held assets, level of internationalization and geographical location (Shah et al., 2009; Meskovic and Zaimovic, 2021).

As it turns out, a high level of risk management maturity, as diagnosed by performed measurements, can have a number of positive consequences for an enterprise's position. These include, for example, greater management commitment, the creation of an Enterprise Risk Management culture, the integration of risk management into the enterprise's strategy and operational plans, an excellent ability to uncover risk dependencies and correlations across the entire enterprise. All these outcomes combined lead to increased company value when undertaking the Enterprise Risk Management maturity journey ceteris paribus (Farrell and Gallagher, 2015), which is a compelling argument for cyclical, precise and continuously improved measurement of an enterprise's risk management maturity based on a set of carefully selected attributes.

Due to their specificity and scale of impact on an enterprise's position, crisis situations also constitute a very important reason for measuring risk management maturity. A higher level of risk management maturity, associated with the increasing professionalization and specialization of an enterprise in this area, may in this case contribute to improved management under crisis conditions. Nevertheless, the measurement of risk management maturity that would be adequate for crisis situations should be adapted to their specific character, using such assessment attributes that, on the one hand, can be universally applied in risk management and, on the other hand, are dedicated to crisis situations as different from periods of normal business activities. The combined use of attributes of these two types should allow for diagnosing an enterprise's both preparation for the potential occurrence of a crisis and implementation of measures to neutralize a factual crisis situation or to support its development by taking advantage of opportunities generated by a crisis situation.

In summary, it can be assumed that the sequence of emergence of risk management maturity in crisis situations is as shown in Figure 2.1.

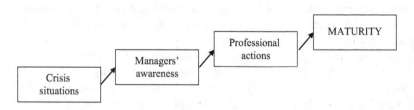

Figure 2.1 A sequence of the emergence of risk management maturity in crisis situations.

Source: the authors' own work.

References

Abdelnour, A., Babbitz, T., Moss, S. (2020). Pricing in a pandemic: Navigating the COVID-19 crisis, www.mckinsey.com/business-functions/marketing-and-sales/our-insights/pricing-in-a-pandemic-navigating-the-covid-19-crisis (Access: 2.12.2021).

Bayazit, Z.D., Cengel O., Tepe, F.F., (2003). Crisis Management in Organizations and a Case Study. 11th National Management and Organization Congress Leaflet of Notices. Afyon, pp. 366–377. www.worldcat.org/title/11-ulusal-yonetim-ve-organizasyon-kongresi-bildiriler-kitab-22-24-mays-2003-afyon/oclc/123011810

Bigley, G.A., Roberts, K.H. (2001). The incident command system: High-reliability organizing for complex and volatile task environments. *Academy of Management Journal*, 44, pp. 1281–1299.

Bircan, C., De Haas, R., Schweiger, H., Stepanov, A. (2020). Coronavirus credit support: Don't let liquidity lifelines become a golden noose. VOX, CEPR Policy Portal. https://cepr.org/voxeu/columns/coronavirus-credit-support-dont-let-liquidity-lifelines-become-golden-noose (Access: 29.11.2021).

Brockner, J., James, E.H. (2008). Toward an understanding of when executives see crisis as opportunity. *The Journal of Applied Behavioral Science*, 44(1), pp. 94–115.

Bundy, J., Pfarrer, M.D. (2015). A burden of responsibility: The role of social approval at the onset of a crisis. *Academy of Management Review*, 40, pp. 345–369.

Bundy, J., Pfarrer, M.D., Short, C.E., Coombs, W.T. (2017). Crises and crisis management: Integration, interpretation, and research development. *Journal of Management*, 43(6), pp. 1661–1692.

Cener, P. (2007). Crisis Management, pp. 4–5, www.danismend.com/ (Access: 1.12.2021).

Coombs, W.T., Holladay, S.J. (2002). Helping crisis managers protect reputational assets. *Management Communication Quarterly*, 16, pp. 165–186.

Craven, M., Liu, L., Wilson, M., Mysore, M. (2020). COVID-19: Implications for business, www.mckinsey.com/business-functions/risk/our-insights/covid-19-implications-for-business (Access: 2.12.2021).

Ernst & Young (2020). Regulatory risk management for responding to COVID-19 pandemic, https://assets.ey.com/content/dam/ey-sites/ey-com/en_in/topics/covid-19/regulatory-compliance-india-covid-19.pdf (Access: 4.12.2021).

Farrell, M., Gallagher, R. (2015). The valuation implications of enterprise risk management maturity. *The Journal of Risk and Insurance*, 82(3), pp. 625–657.

Fener, T., Cevik, T. (2015). Leadership in crisis management: Separation of leadership and executive concepts. *Procedia Economics and Finance*, 26, pp. 695–701.

Gartner (2020). GC Actions in Response to COVID-19, www.gartner.com/en/legal-compliance/insights/coronavirus-resources (Access: 6.12.2021).

Gephart, R.P., Van Maanen, J., Oberlechner, T. (2009). Organizations and risk in late modernity. *Organization Studies*, 30, pp. 141–155.

Glaesser, D. (2006). *Crisis Management in the Tourism Industry*. Burlington, MA: Elsevier.

Gourinchas, P., Kalemli-Özcan, S., Penciakova, V., Sander, N. (2020). COVID-19 and business failures, www.oecd.org/global-forum-productivity/webin ars/Gourinchas-Kalemli-Ozcan-covid-19-and-business-failures.pdf (Access: 5.12.2021).

Groh, M. (2014). Strategic management in times of crisis. *American Journal of Economics and Business Administration*, 6(2), pp. 49–57.

Hart, P., Heyse, L., Boin, A. (2001). New trends in crisis management practice and crisis management research: Setting the agenda. *Journal of Contingencies and Crisis Management*, 9(4), pp. 181–188.

He, H., Harris, L. (2020). The impact of COVID-19 pandemic on corporate social responsibility and marketing philosophy. *Journal of Business Research*, 116, pp. 176–182.

Hedwall (2020). The ongoing impact of COVID-19 on global supply chains, www.weforum.org/agenda/2020/06/ongoing-impact-covid-19-global-sup ply-chains/ (Access: 4.12.2021).

Jaques, T. (2007). Issue management and crisis management: An integrated, non-linear, relational construct. *Public Relations Review*, 33(2), pp. 147–157.

Jedynak, P., Bąk, S. (2021). *Risk Management in Crisis: Winners and Losers During the COVID-19 Pandemic*. London, New York: Routledge.

Kahn, W.A., Barton, M.A., Fellows, S. (2013). Organizational crises and the disturbance of relational systems. *Academy of Management Review*, 38, pp. 377–396.

Karim, A.J. (2016). The indispensable styles, characteristics and skills for charismatic leadership in times of crisis. *International Journal of Advanced Engineering, Management and Science*, 2(5), pp. 363–372.

Koulouridi, S., Kumar, S., Nario, L., Pepanides, P., Vettori, M. (2020). Managing and monitoring credit risk after the COVID-19 pandemic, www.mckinsey. com/business-functions/risk/our-insights/managing-and-monitoring-credit-risk-after-the-covid-19-pandemic (Access: 2.12.2021).

Krystek, U. (1987). *Unternehmungskrisen. Beschreibung, Vermeidung und Bewältigung Überlebenskritischer Prozesse in Unternehmungen*. Wiesbaden: Gabler.

Li, J-Y., Sun, R., Tao, W., Lee, Y. (2021). Employee coping with organizational change in the face of a pandemic: The role of transparent internal communication. *Public Relations Review*, 47(1), 101984.

Litovchenko, Y. (2012). The choice and justification the strategy of enterprise crisis management. *Biznes Inform*, 12, pp. 308–312.

Maurin L., Pál, R., Revoltella, D. (2020). EU firms in the post-COVID-19 environment. VOX, CEPR Policy Portal. https://cepr.org/voxeu/columns/eu-firms-post-covid-19-environment-investment-debt-trade-offs-and-optimal-sequencing (Access: 29.11.2021).

Meskovic, M.N., Zaimovic, A. (2021). Risk management maturity, its determinants and impact on firm value: Empirical evidence from joint-stock companies in Bosnia and Herzegovina. *South East European Journal of Economics and Business*, 16(2), pp. 132–149.

Mikušová, M., Horváthová, P. (2019). Prepared for a crisis? Basic elements of crisis management in an organisation. *Economic Research-Ekonomska Istraživanja*, 32(1), pp. 1844–1868.

Mitroff, I. (2004). Think like a sociopath, act like a saint. *Journal of Business Strategy*, 25(4), pp. 42–53.

Ndlela, M.N. (2018). A Stakeholder Approach to Risk Management. [in:] M.N. Ndlela, *Crisis Communication*. Cham, UK: Palgrave Macmillan, pp. 53–75.

Pearson, C.M., Clair, J.A. (1998). Reframing crisis management. *Academy of Management Review*, 23, pp. 59–76.

Richter, A., Wilson, T.C. (2020). COVID-19: Implications for insurer risk management and the insurability of pandemic risk. *The Geneva Risk and Insurance Review*, 45, pp. 171–199.

Shah, L., Siadat, A., Vernadat, F. (2009). Maturity assessment in risk management in manufacturing engineering. 3rd Annual IEEE Systems Conference, Vancouver, BC, Canada, March 2009.

Shayb, H.A. (2017). Crisis management versus risk management – a practical approach. *Internal Auditing and Risk Management*, 46(2), pp. 28–35.

Shiller, R.J. (2012). *The Subprime Solution: How Today's Global Financial Crisis Happened and What to Do About It*. 1st Edn., Illustrated, Princeton: Princeton University Press.

Sienkiewicz-Małyjurek, K. (2015). *Skuteczne zarządzanie kryzysowe*. Warszawa: Difin.

Slatter, S., Lovett, D. (2001). *Restrukturyzacja firmy. Zarządzanie przedsiębiorstwem w sytuacjach kryzysowych*. Warszawa: WIG-Press.

Splett, M. (2020). Ubezpieczenia ryzyk cybernetycznych oraz policy crime w świetle COVID-19, www.marsh.com/pl/pl/insights/risk-in-context/cyber-crime-COVID-19.html (Access: 6.12.2021).

Starbuck, W.H., Milliken, F.J. (1988). Challenger: Fine tuning the odds until something breaks. *Journal of Management Studies*, 25, pp. 319–340.

Thürmer, J.L., Wieber, F., Gollwitzer, P.M. (2020). Management in times of crisis: Can collective plans prepare teams to make and implement good decisions?. *Management Decision*, 58(10), pp. 2155–2176.

Unctad (2020). World Investment Report 2020: International Production beyond the Pandemic. United Nations Publications, Geneva, https://unctad.org/system/files/official-document/wir2020_en.pdf (Access: 5.12.2021).

Wang, W.T., Belardo, S. (2005). Strategic integration: A knowledge management approach to crisis management. Paper presented at the 2014 47th Hawaii International Conference on System Sciences, 8, Big Island, Hawaii, 252a.

Wenzel, M., Stanske, S., Lieberman, M.B. (2020). Strategic responses to crisis. *Strategic Management Journal*, 41, pp. 7–18.

Zelek, A. (2003). *Zarządzanie kryzysem w przedsiębiorstwie. Perspektywa strategiczna*. Warszawa: Instytut Organizacji i Zarządzania w Przemyśle 'Orgmasz'.

Ziarko, J., Walas-Trębacz, J. (2010). *Podstawy zarządzania kryzysowego*. Kraków: Krakowskie Towarzystwo Edukacyjne – Oficyna Wydawnicza AFM.

3 Research methodology

3.1 Research objectives and questions

We conceptually divided the research process into the following stages: (1) identification of a research gap, (2) formulation of research objectives and questions, (3) development of the authors' original model of risk management maturity, (4) targeted selection of enterprises to be researched and sources of empirical data, (5) performance of the research, (6) validation of the developed model (assessment of risk management maturity of the selected enterprises in the years 2018 and 2020), (7) diagnosis of changes in risk management maturity in the enterprises under analysis in the aftermath of the COVID-19 pandemic and their implications for the management of these enterprises.

In view of the identified research and literature gap regarding the lack of a model for assessing risk management maturity that takes into account the specifics of crisis situations, we formulated two key research objectives: one oriented towards theory development and the other related to practical applications. The former concerned the building of a new multidimensional model for assessing risk management maturity, adapted to the specifics of crisis situations such as the COVID-19 pandemic, while the latter was about the validation of the proposed model in selected enterprises listed on the Warsaw Stock Exchange and representing the sectors of financial services, construction and IT. In conjunction with the research objectives, we posed the following research questions:

- What attributes should be taken into account in order to make a reliable assessment of the risk management maturity of enterprises operating under crisis conditions?
- Has the risk management maturity of the examined enterprises changed in the aftermath of the COVID-19 pandemic, and if so, for which attributes has a change been observed?

DOI: 10.4324/9781003330905-4

- How should the developed model of assessing risk management maturity be used so that it manifests utilitarian qualities in the practice of business management?

3.2 Research methods

In order to meet the research objectives and answer the research questions, we used a triangulation of research methods (Denzin, 1970; Flick, 2018). Qualitative research methods played a dominant role in our work. The primary method used to build a risk management maturity model was the morphological analysis method (Zwicky, 1966, 1972; Trocki and Wyrozębski, 2014). According to the methodological rigour of this method (Zwicky, 1966, Müller, 2013), the model building process was divided into the following phases:

- defining the problem,
- identifying the problem variables, i.e. the main elements determining the solution of the problem, and establishing their values (in our case – developing a catalogue of attributes and scales illustrating the values they take),
- compiling and arranging the problem variables (in our case – the attributes) and the values corresponding to the variables (in our case – the scales of the values taken by the attributes) in the form of a table referred to as a morphological matrix,
- creating variants of solutions to the problem by combining the relevant variants of the problem variables (in our case – developing a combined scale of risk management maturity),
- evaluating the developed variants of solutions (in our case – measuring the maturity of risk management in the enterprises under analysis based on the assumptions of the model).

A graphical representation of the model building process is shown in Figure 3.1.

Developing a catalogue of attributes in our model, we used the technique of exploratory research (Saunders et al., 2009). We defined the attributes based on a review of the existing models and the current literature on the subject, recognizing the need to broaden and refine their scope in adjustment to crisis situations. Creating a measurement scale for assessing the level of risk management maturity, we applied the adaptation approach to scale development in management research (Farh et al., 2006), which involves modifying the already existing scales to create a more meaningful version. During the validation of our model

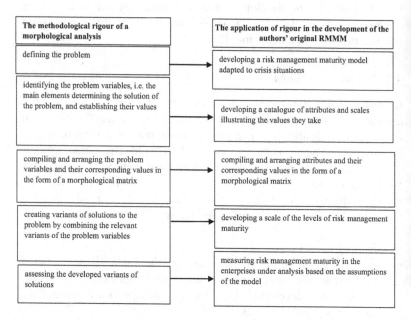

Figure 3.1 The application of the methodological rigour of a morphological analysis in the development of a new risk management maturity model.

Source: the authors' own work.

we followed the data-oriented validation approach, specific to the validation of models in management, based on the important role of empirical data in the validation practice in all main areas of science (Eker et al., 2018). This approach enabled us as researchers to validate the model in terms of the external evaluation of risk management maturity of the enterprises participating in the research. Validating the model, we also used a multiple case study combining a descriptive variant and an exploratory variant (Yin, 2003). As regards the exploratory variant, we used exemplification (Kaźmierska, 2018), testing our model on the selected enterprises. We tested the model for the following two periods: 2018 (before the pandemic) and 2020 (during the pandemic). For this purpose, we used the comparative analysis method (Esser and Vliegenthart, 2017) in the closed comparison variant, where entities to be compared are selected a priori, before the beginning of a research project (Konecki, 2000). They are compared over time, intra- and intersectorally, with respect to the majority of their respective risk management systems. Applying the descriptive multiple case study variant, we used the method of analysing the content of the source documentation (Bowen, 2009) generated in the enterprises participating in the research in order to reliably assess the individual attributes of our model in the enterprises. Furthermore, in order to make a final diagnosis of the impact of the COVID-19 pandemic on risk management maturity of the examined enterprises, we used a qualitative data analysis (Gibbs, 2021), including excerpts from the enterprises' corporate documents (citations) confirming specific changes in the assessment of the individual attributes caused by the COVID-19 pandemic. For this purpose, we coded the data, using the MAXQDA Analytics Pro 2022 software. We used grounded coding, based on observations made during the course of the research and the obtained research material. It took the form of hierarchical coding, i.e. multi-level coding based on the extraction of the main categories of codes together with the sub-categories assigned to them. The coding approach adopted by us was data driven coding, that is coding based on a close relationship with data and providing for the incremental generation of analytical conclusions (Gibbs, 2007, 2021).

According to methodological rigour, we divided the coding process into the following stages:

- preparing data for coding (selecting citations from the source documents of the examined enterprises and assigning them to the enterprises based on the adopted numbering within the sectors under examination),
- preparing us (the authors of the monograph) as coders for coding,
- conducting the first coding cycle (either co-author of the monograph independently conducted the process of coding the citations selected from the enterprises' documentation),
- we prepared the codebook,
- the second coding cycle (on the basis of the codes established by us independently, we identified common codes on the basis of the substantive relationships between the codes established by us independently – we qualified 78 common codes for further analysis),
- the codes were prioritized and categorized, creating a code tree (whereby we organized the codes, created code bundles and hierarchical categories):
  - we created five main categories of codes,
  - within each of the five main categories of codes, we identified three subcategories, following the principle of separability and exhaustiveness of the created subcategories,

Table 3.1 The enterprises selected for the research

Sector	Sub-sector	Designations of enterprises	Number of enterprises in the sub-sector	Number of enterprises in the sector
Construction (CON)	Construction	CON 1–CON 38	38	38
Financial Services (FS)	Banks	FS 1–FS 12	12	28
	Leasing and factoring	FS 13	1	
	Financial intermediation	FS 14–FS 15	2	
	Capital market	FS 16–FS 21	6	
	Insurance	FS 22–FS 24	3	
	Debt collection	FS 25–FS 28	4	
IT (IT)	Information technology	IT 1–IT 24	24	41
	Media	IT 25–IT 38	14	
	Telecommunication	IT 39–IT 41	3	
Total	–		107	107

Source: Giełda Papierów Wartościowych w Warszawie (2019). www.gpw.pl/spolki (Access: 25.06.2019); Giełda Papierów Wartościowych w Warszawie (2021). www.gpw.pl/spolki (Access: 10.09.2021).

- to each of the subcategories, we assigned specific codes based on their relevance,
- we analysed the relationship between the codes and their categories, and developed explanatory models allowing for an interpretation of research results.

3.3 Data sources

We selected the enterprises for the research by way of targeted election. We decided to validate our model and assess the maturity of risk management in those Polish corporations that had been listed on the main (primary and parallel) market of the Warsaw Stock Exchange on both 25 June 2019 and 10 September 2021 and represented the most numerous sectors of financial services, construction and IT. These criteria were fulfilled by 107 enterprises. Broken down into sectors and sub-sectors, they are presented in Table 3.1.

In the presentation of the research results, we used anonymized names of the enterprises under analysis, presented according to a predetermined key: a sector name abbreviation + an ordinal number: financial services (FS1–FS28), construction (CON1–CON38), IT (IT1–IT41).

In the research, we used triangulation of data sources (Knafl and Breitmayer, 1989) to increase the reliability of the obtained information (Patton, 1990). We assessed maturity based on the enterprises' source documentation for the years 2018 and 2020. The source documents that were used as sources of empirical data together with the number of the enterprises for which we used a particular source are presented in Table 3.2.

Table 3.2 The sources of the empirical data

Empirical data source	Number of enterprises		
	FS	CON	IT
Annual reports (financial statements and operations reports)	28	38	41
Reports on capital adequacy as well as other information and disclosures subject to obligatory announcement by entities listed on the Warsaw Stock Exchange	12	0	0
Non-financial information statements	1	8	1
Corporate governance statements	28	38	41
Integrated reports or sustainability reports	1	5	2

Source: the authors' own work.

44   *Research methodology*

References

Bowen, G.A. (2009). Document analysis as a qualitative research method. *Qualitative Research Journal*, 9(2), pp. 27–40.

Denzin, N.K. (1970). *The Research Act: Theoretical Introduction to Sociological Methods*. Chicago: Aldine Publishing Co.

Eker, S., Rovenskaya, E., Obersteiner, M., Langan, S. (2018). Practice and perspectives in the validation of resource management models. *Nature Communications*, 9, 5359.

Esser, F., Vliegenthart, R. (2017). Comparative Research Methods [in:] J. Matthe (ed.), *The International Encyclopedia of Communication Research Methods*. Hoboken, NJ: John Wiley & Sons, pp. 1–22.

Farh, J-L., Cannella, A.A., Lee, C. (2006). Approaches to scale development in Chinese management research. *Management and Organization Review*, 2(3), pp. 301–318.

Flick, U. (2018). *Doing Triangulation and Mixed Methods*. Thousand Oaks, CA: Sage.

Gibbs, G. (2007). *Analyzing Qualitative Data*. London: Sage.

Gibbs, G. (2021). *Analizowanie danych jakościowych*. Warszawa: PWN.

Giełda Papierów Wartościowych w Warszawie (2019). www.gpw.pl/spolki (Access: 25.06.2019).

Giełda Papierów Wartościowych w Warszawie (2021). www.gpw.pl/spolki (Access: 10.09.2021).

Kaźmierska, (2018). Doing biographical research-ethical concerns in changing social contexts. *Polish Sociological Review*, 3(203), pp. 393–411.

Knafl, K., Breitmayer, B.J. (1989). Triangulation in Qualitative Research: Issues of Conceptual Clarity and Purpose. [in:] J. Morse (ed.), *Qualitative Nursing Research: A Contemporary Dialogue*. Rockville, MD: Aspen, pp. 193–203.

Konecki, K. (2000). *Studia z metodologii badań jakościowych. Teoria ugruntowana*. Warszawa: PWN.

Müller, R. (2013). Morphologie von Goethe bis Zwicky. Strukturbeschreibung, Entdeckungsmethode. Weltansicht. Müller Science.

Patton, M. (1990). *Qualitative Evaluation and Research Methods,* 2nd ed. Newbury Park, CA: Sage.

Saunders, M., Lewis, P., Thornhill, A. (2009). *Research Methods for Business Students*. 5th ed. Harlow: Pearson Education.

Trocki, M., Wyrozębski P. (2014). Zastosowanie analizy morfologicznej w naukach o zarządzaniu. *Organizacja i Kierowanie*, 2(162), pp. 27–44.

Yin, R.K. (2003). *Case Study Research: Design and Methods* (3rd ed.). Thousand Oaks, CA: Sage.

Zwicky, F. (1966). *Entdecken, Erfiden, Forschen im morphologischen Weltbild*. München: Droemer Verlag.

Zwicky, F. (1972). Morphologisches Denken und Vorgehen [in:] *Die neuen Methoden der Entscheidungsfindung*. München: Verlag Moderne Industrie.

4 Development of a new risk management maturity assessment model

4.1 Attributes

Developing our risk management maturity model, we began by establishing a catalogue of attributes to be assessed. We recommend assessing risk management maturity against the following eight attributes: A. Strategy, B. Planning and goals, C. Culture, D. Standards and procedures, E. Processes, F. Roles and responsibilities, G. Compliance, H. Crisis resilience. We chose these attributes, taking into account those present in the existing models (especially the frequency of their occurrence), as well as the specific requirements for risk management that are characteristic of crisis situations. A detailed description of the attributes is presented below.

A Strategy

This attribute concerns maturity at the level of strategic business management. First of all, it refers to the extent to which an enterprise's development strategy takes account of uncertainty and prevailing risks (Sheehan, 2010; Slagmulder and Devoldere, 2018). In formulating a growth strategy, it is important, among other things, to establish whether strategic risks, e.g. business continuity risk, reputation risk, investment risk (Jedynak and Bąk, 2021), have been identified by the enterprise as input in the process of its formulation.

Such features of the adopted development strategy as the occurrence of strategic options, action scenarios and flexibility indicate the fulfilment of the above condition.

A high level of an enterprise's maturity is also indicated by the development of professional strategies dedicated to risk management, in the form of a Risk Management Strategy (Gantz and Philpott, 2013) or strategies relating to specific types of risk, such as an operational risk

DOI: 10.4324/9781003330905-5

management strategy (Qu and Zhang, 2012) or a market risk management strategy (Chakraborty et al., 2021).

Finally, the integration of the management strategies functioning in the enterprise, including risk management strategies, is important for assessing maturity.

B Planning and goals

This attribute concerns the maturity associated with the formulation of an enterprise's goals and plans that take into account the risks associated with its activities.

The formulation of business plans based on risk analyses is one of the indications of a high level of risk management maturity within the enterprise. This is fostered by the use of adequate analytical tools such as the Strengths, Weaknesses, Opportunities, Threats (SWOT) Analysis (Eshaghi et al., 2015), Failure Mode and Effect Analysis (FMEA) (Mandru, 2012) or the Risk Matrix (Thomas et al., 2013).

The form of action plans, which can be characterized by multiple variants and Scenario Planning (Zahradníčková and Vacík, 2014), is also not without significance.

An additional important manifestation of maturity is the drawing up of plans that are particularly oriented towards risk management, for example: Risk Response Plans (Ahmadi-Javid et al., 2020), Risk Mitigation Plans (INCOSE, 2010).

A high level of maturity is also indicated by the formulation of business goals that directly concern risk management. The scope of such goals is also important, i.e. whether they relate solely to ensuring compliance and are of a universal nature or are formulated in relation to risks specific to the sector in which the enterprise operates (Jedynak and Bąk, 2019).

For the assessment of maturity, it is also important to integrate the plans and goals formulated in relation to the identified risks with the overall leading plans of the enterprise.

C Culture

This attribute refers to maturity related to the building of an organizational culture that puts emphasis on taking into account the approach to risk and its management adopted in an enterprise. This is important because the cultural aspects of an organization are closely related to the way in which it perceives risk (Appleby-Arnold et al., 2018).

A tangible manifestation of the existence of such a relationship is that companies build a culture oriented towards risk (Abuzarqa, 2019) in the form of a risk culture (Zeier Roeschmann, 2014; Osman and Lew, 2019).

A high degree of an enterprise's maturity is also evidenced by the presence of a risk-based organizational culture in which the involvement of employees and other stakeholders in risk management constitutes a typical cultural standard.

It is also important to ensure that no conflicts occur between the risk-based culture and the leading management processes in the enterprise (Thomya and Saenchaiyathon, 2015).

D Standards and procedures

This attribute relates to maturity associated with a formalized approach to risk management. It first refers to whether and how risk management rules and processes have been formalized within the enterprise (Brownsword and Setchi, 2011) through the preparation of appropriate internal documents.

These can be general documents (e.g. an investment policy, capital management policy, development policy, anti-corruption policy, personal data protection policy) or documents specifically dedicated to risk management (e.g. policies, procedures and rules of procedure that provide guidance on management processes for different identified risks).

Indeed, formalization and standardization play an important role in first implementing and then improving the effectiveness of risk management (Ciocoiu and Dobrea, 2010).

A high degree of an enterprise's maturity in terms of standards and procedures is also evidenced by the implementation of international and recognized management standards (directly or indirectly) oriented towards risk, such as: ISO 31000, ISO 9001, ISO 45001, ISO 14001, ISO/IEC 27005, ISO 28000, ISO 22301 and ISO 26000.

Another element useful in the assessment of maturity is the implementation of Enterprise Risk Management (ERM), based on numerous dedicated internal documents and all international standards relevant to the sector, fully integrated with other management systems functioning in the enterprise.

E Processes

This attribute relates to the maturity of the planning and implementation of process risk management. At the outset, it is relevant whether recommended risk management processes such as context setting, risk identification, analysis, assessment, handling, recording and reporting, monitoring and review, communication and consultation, as well as improvement are implemented in the enterprise (ISO 31000, 2018). The high degree of the enterprise's maturity in terms of process-based risk management is also evidenced by the advanced level of adaptation of the implemented processes to the specifics of the enterprise and the sector it represents, i.e., for example, basing all processes on key risk factors whose probability of occurrence and expected impact on the enterprise are the highest (The Global Risks Report, 2021).

Cohesion and synergy of all processes implemented as part of risk management, i.e. a systemic approach to process management in a continuous cycle of consecutive activities, are also very important (Jedynak and Bąk, 2021).

F Roles and responsibilities

This attribute refers to maturity associated with the distribution of responsibility for risk management within the enterprise. It primarily concerns whether risk management roles and responsibilities have been established.

This is because it is believed that risk management should be underpinned by an organizational structure that ensures that planning, operational and monitoring activities are adequately coordinated (Karanikas, 2014).

Responsibility for risk management can be left solely in the hands of top management (Aven, 2016) in the form of management and supervisory boards whose main tasks include the following: exercising comprehensive control risk management processes, establishing a risk management strategy, ensuring the smooth operation of the developed risk management system, overseeing the risk management system, assessing the adequacy and effectiveness of the system, as well as overseeing the compliance of the risk management policies and procedures with the enterprise's strategy and plans.

However, a more mature approach consists in delegating responsibility form some of the tasks to representatives of lower hierarchical levels (Jedynak and Bąk, 2020).

The maturity of the enterprise is also determined by the degree of specialization and professionalization in the area of risk management. The implementers of the top management's risk management guidelines can be managers and employees of the existing typical departments within the organizational structure (Knight, 2010), e.g. the finance, controlling or internal audit department. However, these tasks can also be fulfilled by risk management professionals representing risk committees, units, divisions or departments, which are typically headed by risk managers, risk leaders or Chief Risk Officers (Lu et al., 2012; Ertac and Gurdal, 2012; Jedynak and Bąk, 2020). For assessing maturity, it is also important to consider the role of external stakeholders in building accountability for risk management.

G Compliance

This attribute relates to maturity at the compliance level, i.e. the integration of external requirements and internal regulations into risk management processes.

It first concerns whether the enterprise identifies and complies with the applicable requirements included in external legal regulations. Such regulations include, among others: relevant national laws, international laws, guidelines of supervisory authorities, requirements of regulated markets on which the enterprise operates (Bąk, 2018).

The degree of maturity with respect to ensuring compliance is also indicated by the degree of fulfilment of risk management requirements established by the enterprise within its own internal regulations (policies, procedures, rules, etc.).

Another important maturity assessment factor is the functioning of a relevant compliance assurance mechanism in the enterprise, e.g. a compliance management system – CMS (Gammisch and Balina, 2014; Coglianese and Nash, 2020) or an equivalent solution whose basis of operation is the inclusion of compliance risk in the catalogue of identified risk and its active management.

H Crisis resilience

This attribute pertains to maturity in terms of the degree of the enterprise's preparation for a potential crisis, related to the shaping of its resilience to crisis situations. Indeed, such resilience is a determinant of the enterprise's ability to recover from a crisis when it actually occurs (Xiao and Cao, 2017; Ma et al., 2018).

If the condition of a high degree of maturity related to resilience is to be fulfilled, i.e. if the enterprise is to acquire characteristics of resilience, it is necessary to apply concepts that constitute the basis of a business crisis resilience model such as business continuity and disaster resilience (Jedynak and Bąk, 2021).

To implement the above concepts, enterprises can use the following tools: Early Warning Systems, Business Continuity Plans, Disaster

Recovery Plans (Jedynak and Bąk, 2021), crisis scenarios and contingency plans (Richter and Wilson, 2020). Their implementation is a sign of a high degree of maturity of the enterprise in terms of crisis preparedness.

The integration of resilience-building activities of the enterprise focused on the formation of a culture of preparedness is another element particularly important for the assessment of maturity (Carmeli and Schaubroeck, 2008; Kapucu, 2008).

4.2 Morphological Matrix

The next step in the process of building a multidimensional risk management maturity model was developing value scales for each attribute, which we did by applying the rigour of a morphological analysis. The result of this activity is the preparation of the Morphological Matrix, presented in Table 4.1.

The Morphological Matrix comprises eight attributes and five-point scales of values that can be attached to them. The value scales are graded and therefore represent an increasing degree of an enterprise's professionalization in its approach to each of the areas that undergo assessment. Thus, the matrix makes it possible to assess, firstly, the advancement of the enterprise's activities relating to each attribute and, secondly and ultimately, the level of risk management maturity represented by the enterprise.

4.3 Maturity levels

In the next step of building the model, we developed an aggregate risk management maturity assessment scale taking into account the sum of points that the examined enterprises could receive as a result of the assessment of each attribute. Based on the developed assessment scale, we distinguished five levels of risk management maturity: fragmentary, basic, completed, professional and superb. The scale is presented in Table 4.2.

If the established criteria are used, the maturity assessment scale allows for the assessment of the risk management maturity level of any enterprise, from the fragmentary level (reflecting only scarce, selective evidence of the enterprise's approach to risk management), through the intermediate basic, completed and professional ones (indicating increasing maturity and therefore gradual professionalization of the approach to risk management), to the superb one (reflecting the highest maturity of risk management, which is performed in full integration

Table 4.1 Morphological Matrix

Attributes	Attribute values				
	1	2	3	4	5
A: Strategy	A1: Including uncertainty and risk in the strategy to a slight degree	A2: Identifying strategic risks and integrating them into the strategy	A3: Formulating strategic options and action scenarios; ensuring the flexibility of the strategy	A4: Formulating professional strategies dedicated to risk management	A5: Providing full integration of general management and risk management strategies
B: Planning and goals	B1: The enterprise's plans take little account of risk	B2: The enterprise's plans are based on risk analysis – they are characterized by multiple variants	B3: Plans specifically oriented towards risk management have been formulated Risk management goals relate only to compliance	B4: Goals relating to risk management have been formulated, taking into account the specifics of the sector	B5: Full integration of business plans and goals relating to risk management
C: Culture	C1: An organizational culture with little focus on risk management	C2: Selected components of the organizational culture (e.g. standards, values) are oriented towards risk management	C3: A risk culture has been built	C4: A risk culture involving stakeholders	C5: Full alignment between the enterprise's risk culture and management processes
D: Standards and procedures	D1: A low level of risk management formalization	D2: The presence of risk management issues in general documents	D3: Drawing up documents dedicated to risk management Introducing few external risk management standards	D4: Introducing many external risk management standards	D5: An integrated risk management system

(continued)

Table 4.1 Cont.

Attributes	Attribute values				
	1	2	3	4	5
E: Processes	E1: Few processes incorporating risk management	E2: Implementing most risk management processes	E3: Implementing all risk management processes recommended by international standards	E4: Aligning the risk management processes with the sector's specifics and key risk factors	E5: Holistic, systemic approach to the risk management processes
F: Roles and responsibilities	F1: Few examples of defining responsibilities for risk management	F2: Clearly defining managers' responsibilities for risk management	F3: Clearly defining responsibilities for risk management at different levels of the hierarchy	F4: Professional positions and departments responsible for risk management	F5: Synergy of responsibilities for risk management taking into account the role of external partners
G: Compliance	G1: Partially identifying external requirements	G2: Fully identifying external requirements	G3: Ensuring compliance with external and internal requirements	G4: A professional compliance management system or its equivalent	G5: Continuous improvement of compliance practices
H: Crisis resilience	H1: Few characteristics of crisis resilience	H2: Applying selected concepts of developing crisis resilience	H3: Applying concepts and implementing tools related to crisis resilience development	H4: Implementing a culture of preparedness	H5: Organizational learning to improve crisis resilience

Source: the authors' own work.

Table 4.2 The aggregate risk management maturity assessment scale

Maturity level	Description	Score
1 – Fragmentary	There is sparse, selective evidence of taking account of risk in management.	1–8
2 – Basic	The basic functions of risk management are performed.	9–16
3 – Completed	The used risk management approach meets all of internal and external requirements.	17–24
4 – Professional	The approach to risk management exceeds the main requirements and standards and is applied professionally.	25–32
5 – Superb	Risk management is carried out in an integrated manner, is being continuously improved and can act as a benchmark for other organizations.	33–40

Source: the authors' own work.

with the enterprise's management system and optimized through continuous improvement).

The fragmentary maturity level is represented by enterprises that take account of risk in their business management in a negligible and incidental way. They implement neither a systemic nor a processual approach to risk management.

The basic maturity level characterizes organizations that, as a matter of fact, do implement basic risk management functions in alignment with major external requirements, but this is done on a discontinuous basis and is not a systemic solution.

The completed maturity level is typical of businesses that processually and cyclically manage identified, analysed and continuously assessed risks. Enterprises at this level also formalize their approach to risk management internally and clearly define responsibilities. Furthermore, they are clearly focused on developing resilience in their risk management process.

The professional maturity level is characteristic of companies that manage risks systemically, in a professional manner going well beyond mandatory external requirements. In addition, they create full risk awareness among their employees and stakeholders and their approach to risk management is adapted to sectoral circumstances. These enterprises are also adequately prepared in terms of management, content and resources to carry out appropriate actions in the event of a crisis.

The superb maturity level is represented by organizations that have a fully formalized and holistic risk management system integrated into all areas of their business activities. Furthermore, all risk management processes are continuously improved based on past experience. These enterprises also use organizational learning to continuously improve their already developed strong resilience to crises or crisis events, which lets them become benchmarks in the area of risk management improvement.

References

Abuzarqa, R. (2019). The relationship between organizational culture, risk management and organizational performance. *Cross-Cultural Management Journal*, 21(1), pp. 13–20.

Ahmadi-Javid, A., Fateminia, S.H., Gemünden, H.G. (2020). A method for risk response planning in project portfolio management. *Project Management Journal*, 51(1), pp. 77–95.

Appleby-Arnold, S., Brockdorff, N., Jakovljev, I., Zdravković, S. (2018). Applying cultural values to encourage disaster preparedness: Lessons from a low-hazard country. *International Journal of Disaster Risk Reduction*, 31, pp. 37–44.

Aven, T. (2016). Risk assessment and risk management: Review of recent advances on their foundation. *European Journal of Operational Research*, 253(1), pp. 1–13.

Bąk, S. (2018). Risk management in enterprises listed on the Warsaw Stock Exchange: the role of formal and legal determinants. *Przedsiębiorczość i Zarządzanie*, XIX, 9(3), pp. 375–391.

Brownsword, M., Setchi, R. (2011). A formalised approach to the management of risk: Process formalisation. *International Journal of Knowledge and Systems Science*, 2(3), pp. 63–80.

Carmeli, A., Schaubroeck, J. (2008). Organisational crisis-preparedness: The importance of learning from failures. *Long Range Planning*, 41(2), pp. 177–196.

Chakraborty, G., Chandrashekhar, R.G., Balasubramanian, G. (2021). Measurement of extreme market risk: Insights from a comprehensive literature review. *Cogent Economics & Finance*, 9(1), 1920150.

Ciocoiu, C.N., Dobrea, R.C. (2010). The Role of Standardization in Improving the Effectiveness of Integrated Risk Management. [in:] G. Nota (ed.), *Advances in Risk Management*. IntechOpen, pp. 1–18.

Coglianese, C., Nash, J. (2020). Compliance Management Systems: Do They Make a Difference? [in:] D.D. Sokol, B. van Rooij (eds), *Cambridge Handbook of Compliance*. Cambridge University Press, University of Pennsylvania, Inst for Law & Econ Research Paper No. 20-35, pp. 1–46.

Ertac, S., Gurdal, M.Y. (2012). Deciding to decide: Gender, leadership and risk-taking in groups. *Journal of Economic Behavior & Organization*, 83(1), pp. 24–30.

Eshaghi, A., Mousavi, S., Eshaghi, A. (2015). The application of SWOT model to compile appropriate strategies for projects risk management in: Fooladtechnic International Company. *Science Journal of Business and Management*, 3(1–2), pp. 26–34.

Gammisch, M., Balina, S. (2014). The effectiveness of compliance management systems – an experimental approach. *Procedia – Social and Behavioral Sciences*, 156, pp. 236–240.

Gantz, S.D., Philpott, D.R. (2013). *FISMA and the Risk Management Framework*. Chapter 13 Risk Management, pp. 329–365. www.sciencedirect. com/science/article/pii/B9781597496414000138 (Access: 19.01.2022)

INCOSE – International Council on Systems Engineering (2010). Risk mitigation planning, implementation, and progress monitoring. INCOSE Systems Engineering Handbook, Version 3.2, pp. 213–225. www.mitre.org/publicati ons/systems-engineering-guide/acquisition-systems-engineering/risk-man agement/risk-mitigation-planning-implementation-and-progress-monitor ing (Access: 19.01.2022)

ISO 31000 (2018). Risk Management – Guidelines. www.iso.org/standard/ 65694.html (Access: 16.01.2022)

Jedynak, P., Bąk, S. (2019). Objectives of risk management in the financial services sector: the perspective of Polish enterprises listed on the Warsaw Stock Exchange. *Journal of Emerging Trends in Marketing and Management*, 1(1), pp. 231–240.

Jedynak, P., Bąk, S. (2020). The Role of Managers in Risk Management, [in:] A. Michałkiewicz, W. Mierzejewska (eds), *Contemporary Organisation and Management. Challenges and Trends*. Łódź: Łódź University Press, pp. 403–416.

Jedynak, P., Bąk, S. (2021). *Risk Management in Crisis: Winners and Losers during the COVID-19 Pandemic*. London, New York: Routledge.

Kapucu, N. (2008). Culture of preparedness: Household disaster preparedness. *Disaster Prevention and Management*, 17(4), pp. 526–535.

Karanikas, N. (2014). An organisational structure based on risk and quality fundamentals. *International Journal of Management*, 2(1), pp. 1–19.

Knight, K.W. (2010). Risk Management is a journey, not a destination, Presentation to the RusRisk/Marsh ISO 31000 Risk management standard: principle and implementation trends, Seminar, Moscow, 2010.

Lu, J., Jain, L.C., Zhang, G. (2012). Risk Management in Decision Making. [in:] J. Lu, L.C. Jain, G. Zhang (eds), *Handbook on Decision Making. Intelligent Systems Reference Library*, 33, Berlin – Heidelberg: Springer, pp. 3–7.

Ma, Z., Xiao, L., Yin, J. (2018). Toward a dynamic model of organizational resilience. *Nankai Business Review International*, 9(3), pp. 246–263.

Mandru, L. (2012). Application of FMEA Method in Risk Management. Conference Proceedings of the 9th International Conference on Science & Education At: Kemerevo State University, Belovo Institute, Russia.

Osman, A., Lew, C.C. (2019). Developing a framework of institutional risk culture for strategic decision-making. *Journal of Risk Research*, 24(9), pp. 1072–1085.

Qu, S., Zhang, Y. (2012). The Strategy of the Operational Risk Management: Connotations of it in Commercial Banks of China. Fifth International Conference on Business Intelligence and Financial Engineering, pp. 205–209. https://ieeexplore.ieee.org/document/6305112/authors (Access: 19.01.2022).

Richter, A., Wilson, T.C. (2020). COVID-19: Implications for insurer risk management and the insurability of pandemic risk. *The Geneva Risk and Insurance Review*, 45, pp. 171–199.

Sheehan, N.T. (2010). A risk-based approach to strategy execution. *Journal of Business Strategy*, 31(5), pp. 25–37.

Slagmulder, R., Devoldere, B. (2018). Transforming under deep uncertainty: A strategic perspective on risk management. *Business Horizons*, 61(5), pp. 733–743.

The Global Risks Report (2021), World Economic Forum, www.weforum.org/reports/the-global-risks-report-2021 (Access: 20.01.2022).

Thomas, P., Bratvold, R.D., Bickel, J.E. (2013). The risk of using risk matrices. *SPE Economics and Management*, 6(2), pp. 56–66.

Thomya, W., Saenchaiyathon, K. (2015). The effects of organizational culture and enterprise risk management on organizational performance: A conceptual framework. *International Business Management*, 9(2), pp. 158–163.

Xiao, L., Cao, H. (2017). Organizational resilience: The theoretical model and research implication. *ITM Web of Conferences*, 12(18), 04021.

Zahradníčková, L., Vacík, E. (2014). Scenarios as a strong support for strategic planning. *Procedia Engineering*, 69, pp. 665–669.

Zeier Roeschmann, A. (2014). Risk culture: What it is and how it affects an insurer's risk management. *Risk Management and Insurance Review*, 17(2), pp. 277–296.

5 Validation of a new risk management maturity assessment model

Using the developed model, we assessed the risk management maturity of 107 examined enterprises representing the financial services, construction and IT sectors. The assessment covered two different periods, i.e. the years 2018 and 2020. The detailed results of the assessment are based on the source data and are presented in Tables 5.1, 5.2 and 5.3 given at the end of the chapter. In Figures 5.1, 5.2, 5.3, 5.4, 5.5 and 5.6, we present a synthetic summary of the obtained research results and their changes in the two periods under examination.

5.1 Risk management maturity in the enterprises from the financial services sector (FS)

Figure 5.1 shows the changes in risk management maturity that took place in the examined enterprises from the FS sector between 2018 and 2020.

The data presented in Figure 5.1 show that, in the case of almost 80% of the FS sector enterprises (22 out of the 28 enterprises), the total risk management maturity score (the total number of points gained) was higher in 2020 compared to that of 2018, while in only one of these 22 cases the increase in the total score resulted in a change in the maturity level (from professional to superb). It is also worth noting that the high level of advancement in risk management activities in these enterprises was confirmed by the high maturity levels obtained. In 2018, 12 out of 28, and in 2020, 13 out of 28 examined companies in this sector obtained the superb maturity level. However, the dominant maturity level in this sector (in both analysed periods) was the professional level (in 2018, 15 enterprises reached this level, and 14 enterprises in 2020). The lowest maturity in this sector, i.e. the completed level, was achieved by only one analysed enterprise (both in 2018 and 2020). Taking into account the division of the financial services sector into sub-sectors, the

DOI: 10.4324/9781003330905-6

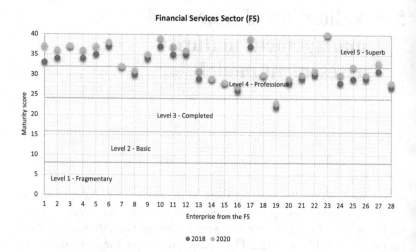

Figure 5.1 A summary of the results of the risk management maturity assessment of the examined enterprises from the FS sector.

Source: the authors' own work.

research showed that the highest risk management maturity level was characteristic of banks (FS1–FS12). As many as 10 of the 12 analysed banks in both study periods were assessed as having achieved the superb maturity level.

Figure 5.2 shows a graphical representation of the results of the conducted research in the FS sector in terms of changes in the assessment of the individual attributes.

The FS sector enterprises achieved the highest level of risk management maturity of all the enterprises covered by the research (in comparison to the enterprises representing the CON and IT sectors). The total sum of the averaged scores of the individual attributes in both examined periods was higher than 30 in this sector (31.5 and 32.9 for the years 2018 and 2020, respectively). The obtained results also confirm an improvement in attribute ratings in 22 of the 28 companies representing the financial sector, which is a trend similar to that observed in the case of the total maturity assessment discussed earlier. Positive changes occurred the most often with respect to attribute H. Crisis resilience (in 21 out of the 22 enterprises) and attribute G. Compliance (in seven out of 22 enterprises). In contrast, positive changes were observed less frequently in the case of attribute C. Culture (in four out of the

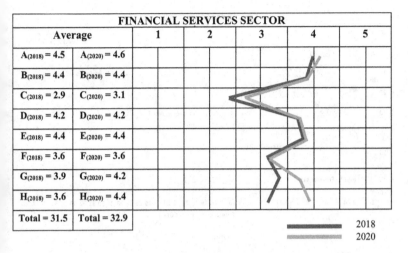

FINANCIAL SERVICES SECTOR						
Average		1	2	3	4	5
$A_{(2018)}$ = 4.5	$A_{(2020)}$ = 4.6					
$B_{(2018)}$ = 4.4	$B_{(2020)}$ = 4.4					
$C_{(2018)}$ = 2.9	$C_{(2020)}$ = 3.1					
$D_{(2018)}$ = 4.2	$D_{(2020)}$ = 4.2					
$E_{(2018)}$ = 4.4	$E_{(2020)}$ = 4.4					
$F_{(2018)}$ = 3.6	$F_{(2020)}$ = 3.6					
$G_{(2018)}$ = 3.9	$G_{(2020)}$ = 4.2					
$H_{(2018)}$ = 3.6	$H_{(2020)}$ = 4.4					
Total = 31.5	Total = 32.9					

2018
2020

Figure 5.2 Averaged assessment scores of the attributes examined in the FS sector enterprises.
Source: the authors' own work.

22 enterprises), A. Strategy (in three out of the 22 enterprises) and B. Planning and goals (in one of the 22 enterprises).

5.2 Risk management maturity in the enterprises from the construction sector (CON)

Figure 5.3 shows the changes in risk management maturity that took place in the examined enterprises from the CON sector between 2018 and 2020.

The results showed that the changes observed in the attributes undergoing assessment resulted in the improvement of risk management maturity in only 8% of the analysed enterprises representing this sector (3 out of the 38 enterprises). In two of the three cases, this was a change from the level of completed to that of professional, and in the third case from professional to superb. The dominant maturity level in this sector was the professional level (in the year 2018 in 17 out of the 38 enterprises, and in 2020 – in 18 of them).

Figure 5.4 shows a graphical representation of the results of the conducted research in the CON sector in terms of changes in the assessment of the individual attributes.

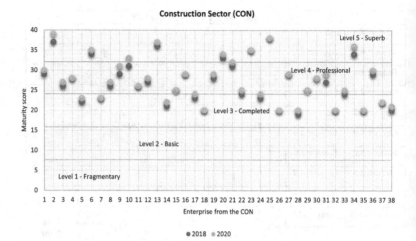

Figure 5.3 A summary of the results of the risk management maturity
assessment of the examined enterprises from the CON sector.

Source: the authors' own work.

CONSTRUCTION SECTOR		1	2	3	4	5
Average						
$A_{(2018)}$ = 3.6	$A_{(2020)}$ = 3.6					
$B_{(2018)}$ = 3.9	$B_{(2020)}$ = 3.9					
$C_{(2018)}$ = 2.7	$C_{(2020)}$ = 2.7					
$D_{(2018)}$ = 3.4	$D_{(2020)}$ = 3.4					
$E_{(2018)}$ = 3.5	$E_{(2020)}$ = 3.5					
$F_{(2018)}$ = 2.9	$F_{(2020)}$ = 3.0					
$G_{(2018)}$ = 3.6	$G_{(2020)}$ = 3.6					
$H_{(2018)}$ = 3.4	$H_{(2020)}$ = 3.9					
Total = 27.0	**Total = 27.6**					

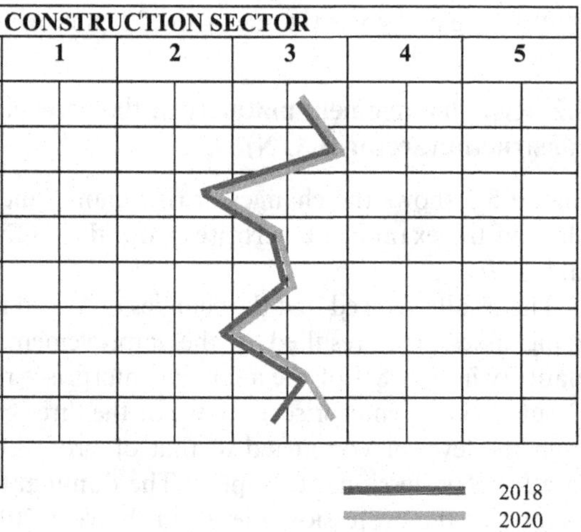

2018
2020

Figure 5.4 Averaged assessment scores of the attributes examined in the CON
sector enterprises.

Source: the authors' own work.

According to the research results, the risk management maturity of the enterprises representing the CON sector did not change significantly in 2020 in comparison to that of 2018 (the average total score was 27.0 and 27.6 for the years 2018 and 2020, respectively). The assessment results of the individual attributes indicate that if there were any changes in their evaluation over time (this happened in the case of 23 out of the 38 examined enterprises), these changes were positive and most often concerned attribute H. Crisis resilience (in 21 out of the 23 cases). Changes also occurred in the assessment of attribute F. Roles and responsibilities (in three out of the 23 cases). The risk management maturity in the CON sector increased also with respect to attributes B. Planning and goals (in two out of the 23 cases), as well as A. Strategy and C. Culture (in one of the 23 cases).

5.3 Risk management maturity in the enterprises from the IT sector (IT)

Figure 5.5 shows the changes in risk management maturity that took place in the examined enterprises from the IT sector between 2018 and 2020.

In the overwhelming majority of cases, the maturity of the analysed enterprises representing the IT sector was assessed as completed. In

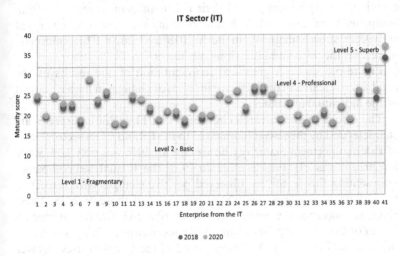

Figure 5.5 A summary of the results of the risk management maturity assessment of the examined enterprises from the IT sector.

Source: the authors' own work.

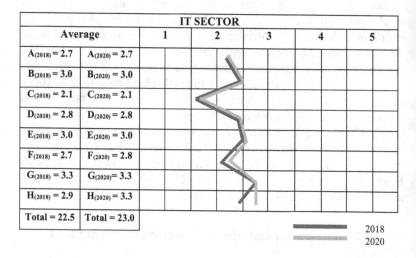

| | IT SECTOR | | | | |
Average	1	2	3	4	5
$A_{(2018)}$ = 2.7 $\quad$ $A_{(2020)}$ = 2.7					
$B_{(2018)}$ = 3.0 $\quad$ $B_{(2020)}$ = 3.0					
$C_{(2018)}$ = 2.1 $\quad$ $C_{(2020)}$ = 2.1					
$D_{(2018)}$ = 2.8 $\quad$ $D_{(2020)}$ = 2.8					
$E_{(2018)}$ = 3.0 $\quad$ $E_{(2020)}$ = 3.0					
$F_{(2018)}$ = 2.7 $\quad$ $F_{(2020)}$ = 2.8					
$G_{(2018)}$ = 3.3 $\quad$ $G_{(2020)}$ = 3.3					
$H_{(2018)}$ = 2.9 $\quad$ $H_{(2020)}$ = 3.3					
Total = 22.5 $\quad$ Total = 23.0					

2018
2020

Figure 5.6 Averaged assessment scores of the attributes examined in the IT
sector enterprises.
Source: the authors' own work.

2018, 30 out of the 41 examined enterprises (73%) achieved this level
of maturity, and in 2020 it was 28 of them (68%). Furthermore, three
examined enterprises improved their risk management maturity from
completed to professional. Only one company in the sector was assessed
as having superb maturity in both 2018 and 2020. This enterprise
represents the telecommunications sub-sector.

Figure 5.6 shows a graphical representation of the results of the
conducted research in the IT sector in terms of changes in the assessment
of the individual attributes.

The results of the research confirmed that IT sector enterprises are
characterized by the lowest (compared to the FS and CON sectors) level
of risk management maturity (the average for 2018 was only 22.5, while
for 2020 it was 23). Furthermore, in 19 of the 41 analysed companies
representing this sector, we observed positive changes with respect to
the individual attributes in 2020 as compared to those of 2018. These
changes concerned the most frequently attribute H. Crisis resilience (in
17 out of the 19 enterprises), while much less frequent changes occurred
in the case of attributes A. Strategy (in 2 of the 19 enterprises), as well
as attributes B. Planning and goals, F. Roles and responsibilities and
G. Compliance (in 1 of the 19 enterprises).

It is also worth emphasizing that the lowest level of maturity that we identified based on the application of our model in all 107 examined enterprises was the completed level. This fact confirms the considerable advancement of their activities undertaken in the area of risk management. No enterprise had their maturity assessed as fragmentary or basic. The reason for these relatively high scores may be the nature of the group under analysis, i.e. companies listed on the Warsaw Stock Exchange, which – due to their presence on the stock market – are obliged to comply with numerous external requirements and standards in shaping their approach to risk.

Table 5.1 Results of the assessment of risk management maturity in the enterprises from the financial services sector (FS)

Attributes	A		B		C		D		E		F		G		H		TOTAL			
																	2018		2020	
Enterprise	2018	2020	2018	2020	2018	2020	2018	2020	2018	2020	2018	2020	2018	2020	2018	2020	Score	Maturity level	Score	Maturity level
FS 1	4	5	4	5	3	3	5	5	5	5	4	4	4	5	4	5	33	5 – Superb	37	5 – Superb
FS 2	4	5	5	5	2	2	5	5	5	5	4	4	5	5	4	5	34	5 – Superb	36	5 – Superb
FS 3	5	5	5	5	5	5	5	5	5	5	4	4	4	4	4	4	37	5 – Superb	37	5 – Superb
FS 4	5	5	5	5	2	3	5	5	4	4	4	4	5	5	4	5	34	5 – Superb	36	5 – Superb
FS 5	5	5	5	5	3	3	5	5	5	5	4	4	4	5	4	5	35	5 – Superb	37	5 – Superb
FS 6	5	5	5	5	5	5	5	5	5	5	4	4	4	4	4	5	37	5 – Superb	38	5 – Superb
FS 7	5	5	4	4	3	3	4	4	4	4	4	4	4	4	4	4	32	4 – Professional	32	4 – Professional
FS 8	4	5	4	4	2	2	4	4	4	4	4	4	4	4	4	4	30	4 – Professional	31	4 – Professional
FS 9	5	5	5	5	2	2	5	5	5	5	4	4	4	4	5	5	34	5 – Superb	35	5 – Superb
FS 10	5	5	5	5	5	5	5	5	5	5	4	4	4	5	4	5	37	5 – Superb	39	5 – Superb
FS 11	5	5	5	5	2	3	5	5	5	5	4	4	5	5	4	5	35	5 – Superb	37	5 – Superb
FS 12	5	5	4	4	3	3	5	5	5	5	4	4	5	5	4	5	35	5 – Superb	36	5 – Superb
FS 13	4	4	4	4	3	4	4	4	4	4	3	3	3	3	4	5	29	4 – Professional	31	4 – Professional
FS 14	4	4	4	4	3	3	4	4	4	4	3	3	4	4	3	3	29	4 – Professional	29	4 – Professional
FS 15	3	3	5	5	2	2	4	4	4	4	3	3	4	4	3	3	28	4 – Professional	28	4 – Professional
FS 16	3	3	4	4	2	2	4	4	4	4	3	3	3	3	3	4	26	4 – Professional	27	4 – Professional

																Sum	Rating	Sum	Rating
FS 17	5	5	5	5	5	5	5	5	5	4	4	4	5	4	5	37	5 – Superb	39	5 – Superb
FS 18	5	5	4	4	2	2	4	4	4	4	4	3	3	3	4	30	4 – Professional	30	4 – Professional
FS 19	3	3	2	2	2	2	3	3	2	2	2	3	3	3	4	22	3 – Completed	23	3 – Completed
FS 20	4	4	4	4	2	2	3	3	4	4	4	4	3	3	4	28	4 – Professional	29	4 – Professional
FS 21	5	5	4	4	2	2	4	4	4	4	4	3	3	3	4	29	4 – Professional	30	4 – Professional
FS 22	5	5	5	4	4	4	3	3	3	3	3	3	3	3	4	30	4 – Professional	31	4 – Professional
FS 23	5	5	5	5	5	5	5	5	5	5	5	5	5	5	5	40	5 – Superb	40	5 – Superb
FS 24	5	5	4	4	2	2	3	3	3	3	3	4	5	3	4	28	4 – Professional	30	4 – Professional
FS 25	5	5	4	3	3	4	3	3	3	3	3	4	5	3	4	29	4 – Professional	32	4 – Professional
FS 26	5	5	4	2	2	3	3	3	3	3	3	3	5	3	4	29	4 – Professional	30	4 – Professional
FS 27	5	5	4	3	3	4	4	4	4	4	4	4	4	4	5	31	4 – Professional	33	5 – Superb
FS 28	3	3	4	3	3	3	3	3	3	3	3	3	3	3	4	27	4 – Professional	28	4 – Professional
Average	4.5	4.6	4.4	4.4	2.9	3.1	4.2	4.2	4.4	3.6	3.6	3.9	4.2	3.6	4.4	31.6	4 – Professional	32.9	5 – Superb

Note: Changes in attribute assessments due to the consequences of the COVID-19 pandemic are highlighted in grey.

Source: the authors' own work.

Table 5.2 Results of the assessment of risk management maturity in the enterprises from the construction sector (CON)

Attributes	A		B		C		D		E		F		G		H		TOTAL			
																	2018		2020	
Enterprise	2018	2020	2018	2020	2018	2020	2018	2020	2018	2020	2018	2020	2018	2020	2018	2020	Score	Maturity level	Score	Maturity level
CON 1	4	4	4	4	2	2	4	4	4	4	3	3	5	5	3	4	29	4 – Professional	30	4 – Professional
CON 2	4	5	5	5	5	5	5	5	5	5	4	4	5	5	4	5	37	5 – Superb	39	5 – Superb
CON 3	4	4	4	5	2	2	3	3	3	3	3	3	3	3	4	4	26	4 – Professional	27	4 – Professional
CON 4	5	5	4	4	3	3	3	3	4	4	3	3	3	3	3	3	28	4 – Professional	28	4 – Professional
CON 5	3	3	4	4	2	2	2	2	2	2	3	3	4	4	3	4	22	3 – Completed	23	3 – Completed
CON 6	5	5	5	5	3	3	5	5	5	5	4	4	4	4	3	4	34	5 – Superb	35	5 – Superb
CON 7	3	3	4	4	2	2	2	2	3	3	2	2	3	3	4	4	23	3 – Completed	23	3 – Completed
CON 8	3	3	4	4	2	4	4	4	3	3	3	3	3	3	4	5	26	4 – Professional	27	4 – Professional
CON 9	3	3	4	4	3	4	4	4	4	4	3	3	4	4	4	5	29	4 – Professional	31	4 – Professional
CON 10	3	3	4	4	4	4	4	4	4	4	3	4	5	5	4	5	31	4 – Professional	33	5 – Superb
CON 11	3	3	4	4	2	2	3	3	3	3	3	3	5	5	3	3	26	4 – Professional	26	4 – Professional
CON 12	5	5	4	4	2	2	4	4	3	3	3	3	3	3	3	4	27	4 – Professional	28	4 – Professional
CON 13	5	5	5	5	4	4	5	5	5	5	3	3	5	5	4	5	36	5 – Superb	37	5 – Superb
CON 14	3	3	4	4	2	2	2	2	2	2	3	3	3	3	2	3	21	3 – Completed	22	3 – Completed
CON 15	3	3	4	4	2	2	3	3	4	4	3	3	3	3	3	3	25	4 – Professional	25	4 – Professional
CON 16	5	5	4	4	3	3	4	4	4	4	3	3	3	3	3	3	29	4 – Professional	29	4 – Professional
CON 17	3	3	4	4	2	2	2	2	3	3	2	2	4	4	3	4	23	3 – Completed	24	3 – Completed
CON 18	3	3	2	2	2	2	2	2	3	3	2	2	3	3	3	3	20	3 – Completed	20	3 – Completed

	1	2	3	4	5	6	7	8	9	10	11	12	13	14	15	16	Σ	Assessment	Σ	Assessment
CON 19	5	5	4	4	2	2	3	3	4	4	3	3	4	4	3	**4**	28	4 – Professional	29	4 – Professional
CON 20	5	5	4	4	3	3	5	5	5	5	3	3	4	4	4	**5**	33	5 – Superb	34	5 – Superb
CON 21	5	5	4	4	4	4	4	4	4	4	3	3	4	4	3	**4**	31	4 – Professional	32	4 – Professional
CON 22	3	3	4	4	2	2	3	3	3	3	3	**4**	3	3	3	3	24	3 – Completed	25	4 – Professional
CON 23	5	5	5	5	4	4	5	5	3	3	4	4	5	5	4	4	35	5 – Superb	35	5 – Superb
CON 24	3	3	4	4	2	2	2	2	3	3	2	2	4	4	3	**4**	23	3 – Completed	24	3 – Completed
CON 25	5	5	5	5	5	5	5	5	5	5	4	4	5	5	4	4	38	5 – Superb	38	5 – Superb
CON 26	2	2	2	2	2	2	3	3	2	2	3	3	2	2	4	4	20	3 – Completed	20	3 – Completed
CON 27	3	3	3	3	4	4	4	4	3	3	4	4	4	4	4	4	29	4 – Professional	29	4 – Professional
CON 28	3	3	2	2	3	3	2	2	2	2	2	2	3	3	3	**4**	19	3 – Completed	20	3 – Completed
CON 29	2	2	4	4	2	2	4	4	3	3	2	2	4	4	4	4	25	4 – Professional	25	4 – Professional
CON 30	5	5	4	4	2	2	3	3	4	4	3	3	4	4	3	3	28	4 – Professional	28	4 – Professional
CON 31	3	3	4	4	2	2	3	**4**	4	4	4	4	3	**4**	4	4	27	4 – Professional	29	4 – Professional
CON 32	2	2	2	2	2	2	2	2	3	3	3	3	3	3	3	3	20	3 – Completed	20	3 – Completed
CON 33	3	3	4	4	2	2	3	3	2	2	4	4	3	3	3	**4**	24	3 – Completed	25	4 – Professional
CON 34	3	3	4	**5**	5	5	5	5	5	5	4	4	5	5	3	**4**	34	5 – Superb	36	5 – Superb
CON 35	2	2	2	2	2	2	3	3	3	3	2	2	3	3	3	3	20	3 – Completed	20	3 – Completed
CON 36	3	3	3	3	3	3	5	5	4	4	3	3	4	4	4	**5**	29	4 – Professional	30	4 – Professional
CON 37	3	3	3	3	2	2	3	3	3	3	2	2	3	3	3	3	22	3 – Completed	22	3 – Completed
CON 38	3	3	3	3	2	2	3	3	3	3	2	2	2	2	2	**3**	20	3 – Completed	21	3 – Completed
Average	3.6	3.6	3.9	3.9	2.7	2.7	3.4	3.4	3.5	3.5	2.9	3.0	3.6	3.6	3.4	3.9	26.9	4 – Professional	27.6	4 – Professional

Note: Changes in attribute assessments due to the consequences of the COVID-19 pandemic are highlighted in grey.

Source: the authors' own work.

Table 5.3 Results of the assessment of risk management maturity in the enterprises from the IT sector (IT)

Enterprise	A 2018	A 2020	B 2018	B 2020	C 2018	C 2020	D 2018	D 2020	E 2018	E 2020	F 2018	F 2020	G 2018	G 2020	H 2018	H 2020	TOTAL 2018 Score	TOTAL 2018 Maturity level	TOTAL 2020 Score	TOTAL 2020 Maturity level
IT 1	3	3	4	4	2	2	3	3	3	3	3	3	3	3	3	4	24	3 – Completed	25	4 – Professional
IT 2	2	2	4	4	2	2	2	2	2	2	3	3	3	3	2	2	20	3 – Completed	20	3 – Completed
IT 3	3	3	2	2	2	2	4	4	3	3	4	4	4	4	3	3	25	4 – Professional	25	4 – Professional
IT 4	2	2	2	2	2	2	3	3	3	3	3	3	4	4	3	4	22	3 – Completed	23	3 – Completed
IT 5	3	3	2	2	2	2	3	3	3	3	3	3	3	3	3	4	22	3 – Completed	23	3 – Completed
IT 6	2	3	2	2	2	2	2	2	2	2	2	2	3	3	3	3	18	3 – Completed	19	3 – Completed
IT 7	5	5	4	4	3	3	3	3	4	4	3	3	4	4	3	3	29	4 – Professional	29	4 – Professional
IT 8	3	3	2	2	3	3	3	3	3	3	3	3	3	3	3	4	23	3 – Completed	24	3 – Completed
IT 9	3	3	4	4	2	2	3	3	3	3	3	3	4	4	3	4	25	4 – Professional	26	4 – Professional
IT 10	2	2	2	2	2	2	3	3	2	2	2	2	3	3	2	2	18	3 – Completed	18	3 – Completed
IT 11	2	2	2	2	2	2	2	2	2	2	2	2	3	3	3	3	18	3 – Completed	18	3 – Completed
IT 12	3	3	4	4	2	2	3	3	3	3	3	3	3	3	3	4	24	3 – Completed	25	4 – Professional
IT 13	3	3	3	3	2	2	3	3	3	3	3	3	4	4	3	3	24	3 – Completed	24	3 – Completed
IT 14	3	3	2	2	2	2	3	3	3	3	3	3	3	3	2	3	21	3 – Completed	22	3 – Completed
IT 15	2	2	2	2	2	2	2	2	3	3	2	2	3	3	3	3	19	3 – Completed	19	3 – Completed
IT 16	2	2	4	4	3	3	2	2	3	3	2	2	3	3	2	2	21	3 – Completed	21	3 – Completed
IT 17	2	2	2	2	2	2	2	2	3	3	3	3	3	3	3	4	20	3 – Completed	21	3 – Completed
IT 18	2	2	2	2	2	2	2	2	2	2	3	3	3	3	3	4	18	3 – Completed	19	3 – Completed
IT 19	3	3	4	4	2	2	3	3	3	3	2	2	3	3	2	2	22	3 – Completed	22	3 – Completed
IT 20	2	2	2	2	2	2	2	2	2	2	3	3	3	3	3	4	19	3 – Completed	20	3 – Completed

IT 21	2	2	2	2	2	2	3	3	3	3	3	2	3	3	3	3	20	3 – Completed	20	3 – Completed
IT 22	4	4	4	2	2	3	3	3	3	3	3	3	3	3	3	3	25	4 – Professional	25	4 – Professional
IT 23	3	4	4	2	2	3	3	3	3	3	3	3	3	3	3	3	24	3 – Completed	24	3 – Completed
IT 24	3	4	4	3	3	3	3	3	3	4	4	3	4	3	3	3	26	4 – Professional	26	4 – Professional
IT 25	3	3	3	2	2	2	2	3	3	3	3	3	3	3	3	4	21	3 – Completed	22	3 – Completed
IT 26	3	4	4	2	2	3	3	4	4	3	3	3	3	3	3	4	26	4 – Professional	27	4 – Professional
IT 27	3	4	4	2	2	3	3	4	4	4	5	3	4	3	3	3	26	4 – Professional	27	4 – Professional
IT 28	4	4	4	2	2	3	3	3	3	3	3	3	4	3	3	3	25	4 – Professional	25	4 – Professional
IT 29	3	2	2	2	2	2	2	3	3	3	3	2	3	2	2	2	19	3 – Completed	19	3 – Completed
IT 30	3	3	4	2	2	3	3	3	3	3	3	3	3	3	3	3	23	3 – Completed	23	3 – Completed
IT 31	2	2	2	2	2	3	3	3	3	2	3	2	3	3	3	3	20	3 – Completed	20	3 – Completed
IT 32	2	2	2	2	2	2	2	3	3	2	3	2	3	3	3	3	18	3 – Completed	18	3 – Completed
IT 33	2	2	2	2	2	2	3	3	3	3	3	3	3	2	2	2	19	3 – Completed	19	3 – Completed
IT 34	2	2	2	2	2	3	3	3	3	3	3	2	3	3	3	4	20	3 – Completed	21	3 – Completed
IT 35	2	2	2	2	2	3	3	3	3	3	3	2	3	2	2	2	18	3 – Completed	18	3 – Completed
IT 36	2	2	4	2	2	3	3	3	3	3	3	2	3	3	3	3	22	3 – Completed	22	3 – Completed
IT 37	2	2	2	2	2	2	2	2	3	3	3	3	3	3	3	3	19	3 – Completed	19	3 – Completed
IT 38	3	3	2	3	3	3	3	4	4	4	4	4	3	3	4	5	25	4 – Professional	26	4 – Professional
IT 39	3	5	5	2	2	5	5	5	5	3	4	3	4	3	4	5	31	4 – Professional	32	4 – Professional
IT 40	3	4	4	2	2	3	3	3	3	3	3	4	3	4	3	4	24	3 – Completed	26	4 – Professional
IT 41	4	5	5	3	3	5	5	5	5	5	5	4	5	4	4	5	34	5 – Superb	37	5 – Superb
Average	2.7	2.7	3.0	3.0	2.1	2.1	2.8	2.8	3.0	3.0	2.7	2.8	3.3	3.3	2.9	3.3	22.4	3 – Completed	22.9	3 – Completed

Note: Changes in attribute assessments due to the consequences of the COVID-19 pandemic are highlighted in grey.

Source: the authors' own work.

6 Impact of the COVID-19 pandemic on risk management maturity in the examined enterprises

In the next stage of the research, we further analysed those attributes of our model for which, in each of the studied sectors, the changes observed between 2018 and 2020 were large enough to be reflected in the averaged (by sector) scores for these attributes, namely: (1) attributes A, C, G, H in the FS sector, (2) attributes F, H in the CON sector and (3) attributes F, H in the IT sector. Eventually, the following attributes were qualified for further analysis: A. Strategy, C. Culture, F. Roles and responsibilities, G. Compliance and H. Crisis resilience. We looked for manifestations of the changes observed in their respective areas in the documents of the examined enterprises, which constituted the main sources of empirical data. The quotations from the documents evidencing the aforementioned changes were subjected to a qualitative content analysis using coding.

6.1 Impact of the COVID-19 pandemic on Strategy

Of the enterprises under analysis, the only ones for which we observed significant changes in risk management maturity with respect to the Strategy attribute during the COVID-19 pandemic, compared to the pre-pandemic period, were the few representatives of the FS sector, namely three banks (FS1, FS2 and FS8).

Figure 6.1 shows the main aspects of changes in the examined enterprises' risk management maturity in the context of the Strategy attribute.

In the activities of banks, previous crises preceding the COVID-19 pandemic, such as the global financial crisis of 2007, revealed the necessity of implementing adaptation processes in the sphere of risk management (Ashby, 2011) and improving its maturity in response to the turbulent changes in the environment. As a consequence, the

DOI: 10.4324/9781003330905-7

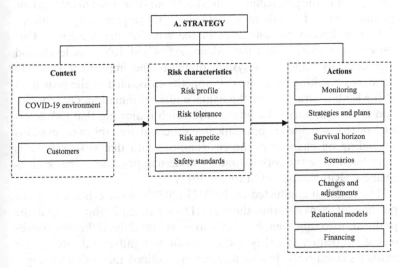

Figure 6.1 Data structure – change in risk management maturity relating to the Strategy attribute.

Source: the authors' own work.

professionalization of risk management was aiming at an ever closer integration of risk management into a leading development strategy.

During the course of our research we observed that the modifications in the banks' strategies were mainly inspired by global macroeconomic changes as a consequence of the pandemic, especially economic lockdowns and other constraints and problems related to the intensification of the risks characteristic of the banking sector, such as liquidity risk or credit risk. Another reason for the implemented changes of a strategic nature in the aftermath of the pandemic, as shown by the results of our research, was the banks' problems in providing services to customers, both individuals and businesses. These problems were mainly related to temporary limitations in customers' solvency and disruptions in their creditworthiness. Identified in our research, the increased risk for banks providing loans during the COVID-19 pandemic was also confirmed by the International Monetary Fund (2020).

As it turns out, the changes of a strategic nature relating to risk management that were introduced in the banks covered by our research were mainly focused on modifications and updates to their risk profiles, based on their existing strategic plans and risk appetite redefined in adjustment to the pandemic. Such adjustments consisted in setting new tolerance levels for individual risks, both those previously unknown and those known but amplified in the wake of the pandemic. Our research also showed that the redefinition of risk tolerance levels had been done by imposing a system of limits and implementing safety standards resulting from the risk appetite embedded in the principles of the leading strategies of the banks under examination. Our conclusion is also supported by previous research indicating that risk tolerance or risk appetite are not static in nature and are subject to revisions depending on changes in the environment, and that risk appetite is considered to be the cornerstone of modern approaches to bank management (Rittenberg and Martens, 2012).

The research conducted by KPMG (2020) on the evolution of the position of banks during the COVID-19 pandemic showed that the problems affecting them had been so severe (mainly in the first phases of the pandemic) that they had often caused significant drops in their market share prices. In our research we noticed that this fact might justify the intensity and scope of countermeasures implemented in the examined banks in response to the circumstances caused by the pandemic. Indeed, our research indicates that they took a number of proactive measures to adapt as much as possible to the new and unprecedented situation. These measures include: conducting more frequent than before and more advanced reviews of current risks, planning and implementing modifying measures, exercising intensive supervision and control, as well as implementing organizational changes appropriate to the situation. They were taken mainly to ensure that strategic objectives were met to the greatest extent possible, despite the problems that occurred as a consequence of the pandemic. One of the banks (FS1) also set a 'survival horizon' during the pandemic, taking into account scenarios of varying severity and likelihood of materialization and analysing the possible impact of each scenario on existing strategic plans and operational effectiveness. Examined banks also undertook a number of activities in the areas specific to the financial services sector. These included, for example: (1) adjusting the principles of credit portfolio valuation and risk parameters to changes in the environment caused by the pandemic, (2) adapting the credit risk management strategy and credit policy to these changes, (3) reconstructing the liquidity profile with a view to maintaining its foundation on stable sources of financing. On many occasions, the activities and measures described above cumulated in the form of redefining the banks' overall strategies, which in one of them (FS8) was described as follows:

This is reflected in the Bank's reconstruction strategy whose important element is the implementation of the relational model, which will, among other things, ensure an increase in the stable sources of funding in the form of cash kept on current and savings accounts of retail customers as well as small and medium-sized enterprises, thus reducing the importance of time deposits in the financing of the Bank.

6.2 Impact of the COVID-19 pandemic on Culture

The few enterprises for which we noted significant changes in risk management maturity with respect to the Culture attribute during the COVID-19 pandemic, compared to the pre-pandemic period, were representatives of the FS sector, including two banks (FS4 and FS11) and two enterprises with a different profile (FS13, FS25).

Figure 6.2 shows the main aspects of changes in the examined enterprises' risk management maturity in the context of the Culture attribute.

In the documents of the analysed enterprises, we found 'traces' indicating the perception of the COVID-19 pandemic as a significant new business condition with a visible potential for impact on cultural issues. In particular, the pandemic was seen as a source of numerous new challenges. It was emphasized (e.g. in FS25) that the pandemic was an unprecedented phenomenon that could hardly be compared to anything preceding it. From this fact, the conclusion was also drawn that

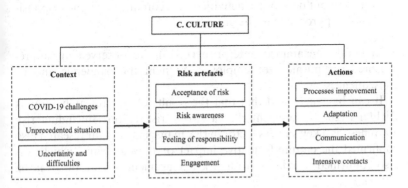

Figure 6.2 Data structure – change in risk management maturity relating to the Culture attribute.

Source: the authors' own work.

since it was an unprecedented phenomenon, it also generated unprecedented difficulties. The analysed enterprises equated such difficulties in particular with unprecedented uncertainty that significantly weakened their ability to predict the impact of the pandemic. The uncertainty caused by the pandemic, and how it differed from other previous crises with a global reach, made it difficult if not impossible for the enterprises to navigate the established management patterns and to use the existing organizational routines. The large number of challenges associated with the pandemic that we confirmed in the examined enterprises was therefore consistent with research conducted by other authors (e.g. Saragih et al., 2021). Shengelia (2021) refers to the pandemic-induced circumstances in which business organizations had to function as 'fundamental uncertainty'.

In the enterprises under examination, we were also able to discern some distinctive cultural artefacts relating to their respective risk cultures rather than generally understood organizational cultures. For example, the managers of one of the banks (FS11) noticed an increase in their employees' awareness of and responsibility for proper risk management at every level of the organizational structure. Under the influence of the pandemic, risk acceptance also began to play an important role, setting a different plane for ongoing decision-making than in the pre-pandemic period. Bank FS4 even drew up an official formula indicating the 'regulatory' role of risk acceptance:

> All Bank employees are required to pay special attention to maintaining the level of risk accepted by the Bank in the process of carrying out day-to-day activities, in accordance with the responsibilities appropriate to the position.

In another examined enterprise (FS25), we observed an unprecedented commitment of employees to fight the pandemic and its consequences.

It can be generalized that that the results of our research support Richter's (2013) statement that a strong risk culture, including risk awareness, is a key success factor in risk management. Our research also confirmed the culture-formative impact of the pandemic, which was also confirmed in relation to a risk management culture by Jivaasha (2021).

The analysed enterprises were taking interesting culture-related measures aimed at bringing the pandemic situation under control. First of all, we can mention the rather original actions of one of the banks (FS11), where an attempt was made to embed process improvement and risk management in the organizational culture more effectively than before. In another enterprise (FS25), even during the pandemic a discussion was initiated about the particular importance of initiating adaptive processes. Many of the enterprises also began to appreciate the role of communication processes, which their managers believed could be an important way of strengthening a risk culture, especially in difficult times such as the COVID-19 pandemic period. One of the more interesting research findings was the discovery of the phenomenon of a significant intensification of the enterprises' contacts with various stakeholders, which indicates a belief in the need for integration and synergy of actions taken to face pandemic challenges. In the case of enterprise FS25, the intensification of contacts occurred, for example, in relation to other business entities and local authorities.

It can therefore be seen that the actions taken in the sphere of culture were largely adaptive in nature and constituted a catalogue of examples typical of the enterprises under analysis. All these actions took place in what Li and Ashkanasy (2019) refer to as a dynamic risk environment.

6.3 Impact of the COVID-19 pandemic on Roles and Responsibilities

We saw significant changes in risk management maturity with regard to the Roles and Responsibilities attribute during the COVID-19 pandemic, compared to the pre-pandemic period, in a few enterprises representing the CON and IT sectors. These were the enterprises coded as CON10, CON22, CON31 and IT40.

Figure 6.3 shows the main aspects of changes in the examined enterprises' risk management maturity in the context of the Roles and Responsibilities attribute.

In the four enterprises mentioned above, several key concerns related to the occurrence of the pandemic emerged. Firstly, the severity of the so-called hard lockdown and its numerous unpredictable consequences were recognized, which could be particularly acute for CON10, a company specializing in the manufacture of building products (mainly paints and varnishes). Secondly, in the same company, two additional risks were identified in the form of a high probability of plant closures, which would constitute a serious threat to the company's existence and a risk directly related to the safety of workers in the workplace. In CON22, on the other hand, attention was drawn to the very dynamic character of the pandemic situation. These findings are in line with the conclusions of the research conducted by Eylemer and Kirkpinar Özsoy (2021), who demonstrated the extremely high vulnerability of

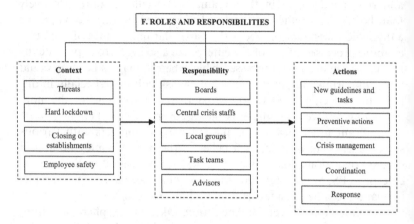

Figure 6.3 Data structure – change in risk management maturity relating to the Roles and Responsibilities attribute.

Source: the authors' own work.

not only individual business organizations but also global economies to the impact of the pandemic and the unreliability of available defence mechanisms. They also correspond with the research of Wilke (2020), who identified the need to redefine worker safety management practices during the pandemic.

The pandemic situation forced the analysed enterprises to make adjustments to their organizational structures, relating to the establishment of specialized posts or organizational units to coordinate risk management activities. In one of the enterprises (CON10), the management board played a key role. In others, it was units such as: central crisis staffs (CON31), local groups (CON31) and also various types of task teams (CON10, IT40). Interestingly, in CON10, specialist crisis management advisors were employed in response to pandemic pressures.

Our research therefore confirms that improving management structures in response to the pandemic, the managers of the analysed enterprises were guided by a sense of responsibility and what Dawson (2020) called a moral obligation to manage risk. Koekemoer et al. (2021) are of the opinion that managers' decisions to improve management structures are a measure of their capacity for leadership during a crisis.

The high level of concretization of responsibility for management during the COVID-19 pandemic in the examined enterprises is reflected in the following excerpts from their official documents in enterprise CON31:

The Group's emergency response preparedness had been tested, however, even before the Plan was developed with the onset of the COVID-19 pandemic. The Group immediately set up a Response Team that operates continuously, managing the pandemic situation at a strategic level,

and in enterprise CON10:

The tasks of the Team include: monitoring the incidence of the disease in the Group and thus managing the risk of increased employee absenteeism, or the possible risk of closure of the Group's plants in specific markets, which could occur, among other things, in the event of a so-called hard lockdown.

In response to the pandemic situation, the enterprises put in place adequate measures within the scope of their roles and responsibilities. To begin with, what deserves mentioning is the preparation of new guidelines and rules of conduct for employees, continuously adjusted to the changing situation (CON10). Furthermore, one enterprise (CON22) initiated and implemented appropriate preventive measures. Obviously, responding to the pandemic, the enterprises were forced to introduce crisis management procedures. Among the measures of primary importance from the point of view of crisis management, they emphasized those aimed at coordination of activities (IT40) and supervision of compliance with the newly introduced rules of conduct (CON10). Ongoing reacting to challenges resulting from the apparent increase in employee absenteeism was also extremely important. All these findings correspond to the results of the research performed by Engelhardt and White (2021). Based on an analysis of several global crises, they cautioned that the biggest threat to enterprises was managers' ignoring the uniqueness of crises and placing too much hope in pre-existing risk management systems.

Also, the conclusions concerning the momentous importance of coordination are similar to those reached by Basak and Zsou (2020), who observed that during the COVID-19 pandemic there was unprecedented coordination of risk-related activities, often forced by enterprises' functioning in numerous global supply chains.

6.4 Impact of the COVID-19 pandemic on Compliance

Among the enterprises for which we noted significant changes in risk management maturity relating to the Compliance attribute during the

COVID-19 pandemic there were seven representatives of the FS sector: three banks (FS1, FS5, FS10), one capital market enterprise (FS17), one insurance enterprise (FS24) and two enterprises in the debt-collection sub-sector (FS25, FS27).

Figure 6.4 shows the main aspects of changes in the examined enterprises' risk management maturity in the context of the Compliance attribute.

The first material reason for the need to improve the maturity of the examined enterprises in the area of compliance was, as our research indicates, the complexity of the situation caused by the COVID-19 pandemic for both the companies and their environment. Another reason that cannot be ignored was the new external legal regulations containing guidelines on the one hand concerning numerous restrictions on the operation of enterprises, and on the other hand imposing new duties and obligations on business organizations. The fact that the key action in response to the global pandemic crisis was the creation of new regulations was also confirmed by the OECD research (2020a), which indicated that such regulations constituted 'the heart of the response to COVID-19'. According to our research, such regulations include, among others, instructions and recommendations of external super-visory institutions such as the European Banking Authority (EBA). The rules defined by the EBA in documents such as: (1) 'Guidelines on

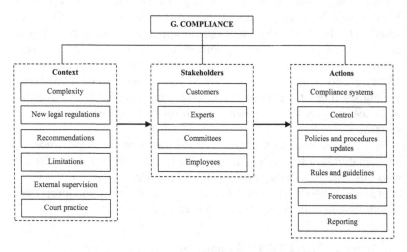

Figure 6.4 Data structure – change in risk management maturity relating to the Compliance attribute.

Source: the authors' own work.

legislative and non-legislative moratoria on loan repayments applied in the light of the COVID-19 crisis' (EBA/GL/2020/02) or (2) amendments to the 'Capital Requirements Regulation (CRR)' fast-tracked in response to the COVID-19 pandemic (EBA/GL/2020/12) had a significant impact on the compliance procedures in the examined enterprises (mainly the FS1 and FS5 banks). Furthermore, in the aftermath of the pandemic, a number of new regulations were introduced at the national level, for example, those developed by the Polish Financial Supervision Authority and applicable to the activities of the enterprises under analysis. Other new important regulations include the amendments to the Polish Commercial Companies Code of 31 March 2020 concerning specific solutions related to preventing, counteracting and combating COVID-19, other infectious diseases and crisis situations caused by them, which document had an impact on the compliance system of the FS17 enterprise. In addition, the circumstances of the COVID-19 pandemic also resulted in changes to judicial practices, for example, in the form of a significant lengthening of ongoing proceedings, which seriously affected the insurance sub-sector enterprise (FS24), whose core business is conducting and participating in pre-litigation and litigation proceedings. To mitigate the risks associated with these changes, this company constantly monitored external changes in the law and the practice of courts, and implemented a strategy to diversify its revenue sources. The research conducted by Marsh (2020) confirms the findings of our study relating to insurance companies, as it shows that the pandemic caused an expansion of insurance services in areas such as property insurance, compensation for cancelled mass events, a dramatically increased cyber risk due to the shift of businesses to the online space, and increased responsibility of managers for the security of their operations and employees, which undoubtedly required insurance companies to increase the maturity of their compliance practices.

The need to ensure compliance with new formal and legal requirements, which intensified in the wake of the COVID-19 pandemic, affected various groups of the examined enterprises' stakeholders, both internal and external ones, forcing them to employ various adaptation measures and more intensive supervisory activities. This primarily affected employees, who had to be additionally trained to ensure compliance during the pandemic crisis. In some of the enterprises under analysis, educational activities were introduced for employees to sensitise them to the risk of third-party access to data and extensive guides/ recommendations were drawn up to address formally cyber security issues. Enterprise FS25 described the process as follows:

In our extensive guide on remote working, we included security principles... We also prepared animated videos on remote working. At the same time, bearing in mind that during the pandemic employees use the Internet more in their both professional and private lives (e.g. shopping), we educated them about potential cyber threats (e.g. phishing).

Thus, the analysed enterprises focused on ensuring business continuity and security while maintaining regulatory compliance under the new hybrid and remote work organization regimes. Besides providing training to all employees, various units in the organizational structure responsible for risk management and beyond were involved in the advanced process of ensuring compliance with the new guidelines during the pandemic. Enterprise FS10 indicated that:

With regard to the credit risk management process, reports and analytical materials on the impact of the pandemic on the quality of the loan portfolio and regulations that adapt credit policies to the changing market situation are presented at the meetings of the Corporate and Investment Banking Risk Committee.

As our research shows, during the COVID-19 pandemic, addressing external regulatory requirements was not the only challenge faced by the examined enterprises in terms of compliance. It turns out that it was also necessary for the enterprises to expand their internal compliance systems by: (1) updating the internal compliance policies and procedures in line with changes caused by the pandemic, or (2) developing completely new rules and guidelines necessary during the pandemic. Taking into account external recommendations, the examined companies updated and improved their internal rules regarding the management of significant risks on an ongoing basis and conducted continuous monitoring of changes to the banking law. They also performed comprehensive quantitative and qualitative analyses on legal, macroeconomic and social issues, continuously tracked developments in the economy and adjusted their credit risk policies on an ongoing basis. One of the capital market enterprises (FS17) even amended its articles of association to comply with the new legislation and drew up regular reviews and reports on the principles and effectiveness of its compliance system, including the results of any audits of compliance issues.

In both implementing external legal requirements arising during the pandemic and developing new internal procedures, it was important for the enterprises to forecast the impact of the pandemic, take into account their customers' perspective and use expert knowledge, which bank FS1 described as follows:

> In the Bank's view, the COVID-19 pandemic represents an unprecedented event and therefore there are significant limitations on the point of reference/benchmark for quantifying the expected course of the macroeconomic deterioration and its impact on customer behaviour. Consequently, the Bank applies an increased scale of expert judgements in the impairment assessment process compared to previous periods. In accordance with the Model Management Policy adopted in the Bank, expert judgements used in the model are objectivized in the process through the use of independent validation and dedicated decision-making levels in the form of the Model Risk Committee and the Bank's Management Board.

In most cases, the examined enterprises presented a holistic adaptive approach to raising the maturity of their compliance systems during the pandemic (the broadest scope of these activities was undertaken by enterprise FS27). To sum up, based on the results of our research, it may be stated that the companies examined by us in this respect pursued a compliance policy comprising ongoing compliance monitoring, testing and adaptation of internal regulations and rules of conduct to the provisions of law, ethical standards and principles of good market practices relevant to the objects of their activity, also taking into account the provisions of anti-corruption, conflict of interest management, compliance risk management and ethical principles. This approach enabled them to avoid a number of serious problems that could have arisen if they had failed to meet the criterion of compliance with the new legal requirements implemented in response to the pandemic. According to the research carried out by Ernst & Young (2020), such problems included trade restrictions resulting in loss of business, additional cost of operations, forceful shutdown of business operations along with fines and penalties levied by the regulators, reputation loss due to negative media reports on failure to adopt preventive or detective measures, damages and compensation to be paid to impacted individuals for not adopting adequate measures, criminal prosecutions against key managerial personnel and/or board members.

6.5 Impact of the COVID-19 pandemic on Crisis Resilience

During the course of our research, we identified clear changes in risk management maturity relating to the Crisis Resilience attribute in the following enterprises: 21 enterprises from the FS sector, 21 enterprises from the CON sector and 17 IT sector representatives, so changes aimed at resilience improvement were the most common among all the examined attributes.

Figure 6.5 shows the main aspects of changes in the examined enterprises' risk management maturity in the context of the Crisis Resilience attribute.

As the results of our research indicate, the COVID-19 pandemic, as well as consequent lockdowns, restrictions and limitations caused a systemic crisis in many companies. This crisis was particularly evident in the entities representing the financial sector. One of the examined banks (FS1) defined a systemic crisis as a situation in which all or a significant part of the banking system experiences liquidity problems due to an economic or financial crisis such as the COVID-19 pandemic. The analysed enterprises also faced increased demands for social responsibility during the pandemic. Many of them indicated that stepping up their social responsibility activities during the pandemic had been the right course of action, which together with sustainability

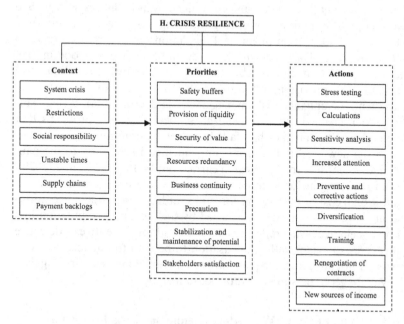

Figure 6.5 Data structure – change in risk management maturity relating to the Crisis Resilience attribute.

Source: the authors' own work.

helped them to build a strong organization resilient to extraordinary risks and challenges. The examined enterprises also stressed that the actions in the area of social responsibility taken during the pandemic had aimed at ensuring the safety of employees, customers, business partners and other stakeholders, as well as ensuring the continuity of business activities. The significant impact of the COVID-19 pandemic on corporate social responsibility is also emphasized in studies other than ours, which confirm that the pandemic triggered marked changes in CSR requirements, assumptions, concepts and practices, particularly as regards stakeholders, societal risk, supply chain responsibility and political economy of CSR (Crane and Matten, 2020).

Financial and non-financial problems occurring in supply chain cooperation, mainly in the international context, were also an important reason why the companies under analysis paid particular attention to building or developing resilience mechanisms. These problems particularly affected the enterprises in the CON sector, which experienced numerous operational problems as a result of pandemic constraints. The analysed enterprises representing this sector (especially CON8, CON12, CON13, CON14, CON19) indicated that these constraints mainly concerned cash flows, payment bottlenecks in supply chains, generation of unforeseen costs, increase in raw material prices, demand constraints, fewer orders, employee absenteeism, problems with physical flows of goods and materials, problems with construction investments, transport constraints, downtime, extended deadlines for obtaining construction administrative decisions and other restrictions imposed by national administrations or EU institutions, which significantly affected their operational functionality and, in particular, ability to meet contractual deadlines. The results of our research supply chain problems caused by the pandemic confirm the findings of other studies in this area, which also clearly indicate that global pandemic-triggered changes significantly disrupted cooperation in supply chains, often interrupting their continuity or dramatically worsening their efficiency and timeliness (Deloitte, 2020).

In general, the COVID-19 pandemic caused instability in the market environment, generating new risk factors requiring the implementation of resilience strengthening measures, also in the case of the IT enterprises analysed in our research (e.g. IT5, IT20). They indicated that these risks had manifested themselves, for example, in the deterioration of the financial standing of customers, the emergence of payment bottlenecks, delayed IT investments, delays in order fulfilment and exchange rate volatility. The identified negative impact of the pandemic on the examined IT enterprises was substantiated by the findings of other studies that highlighted the negative realization of the technological risk during the pandemic, influencing the emergence of numerous financial, infrastructural, legal and organizational barriers to conducting business based on the use of new technologies (OECD, 2020b).

Our research showed that in order to build resilience to the impact of the COVID-19 pandemic crisis, the examined enterprises had decided on several priorities with which specific preventive and corrective measures were aligned. These priorities include the introduction of safety buffers and the provision of liquidity in the process of active financial risk management, despite the occurrence of numerous financial problems. The examined enterprises saw a clear need to adapt liquidity risk management to the environment changed by the pandemic, for example, by: (1) continuously monitoring and frequently reporting on the liquidity situation, (2) exercising extra care in determining the liquidity contingency caused by the unfolding pandemic, (3) including stress conditions in liquidity risk testing scenarios that take into account the effects of a pandemic, (4) determining the required liquidity buffer for external scenarios in regularly conducted analyses, (5) continuously reviewing the adequacy of the COVID-19 scenario assumptions used in stress testing, (6) developing a methodology of calculating and estimating the impact of the pandemic on expected losses in adaptation to the forecast macroeconomic scenarios, (7) performing sensitivity analyses of expected losses against the key assumptions used in the business model, (8) changing the methodology of discounting estimated cash flows.

Another resilience-building priority for the enterprises under analysis was value preservation and resource redundancy. What contributed to the pursuit of these objectives was, among other things, the Supervisory Outlier Test, impairment tests and asset valuation forecasts carried out by the companies representing the FS sector. Among the enterprises from all three sectors, the practices serving to protect value and different groups of assets included the following: (1) creating additional provisions for expected losses to cover uncertainties related to the impact of the pandemic, (2) maintaining replacement resources, (3) postponing expenses that do not determine the continuity of operations, (4) designating critical processes and critical resources and (5) preparing scenarios for the implementation of cost-saving measures.

Another leading objective relating to resilience building during the pandemic was to ensure business continuity. To this end, as indicated by the results of our research, the processes operating during the pandemic were being constantly monitored by means of operational risk tools and the existing principles for identifying crisis phenomena, the scope of actions taken and the scope of responsibility, necessary for both the implementation of preventive measures (i.e. mitigation of risks associated with the pandemic, where it was possible to protect against its negative effects) and the immediate preparation and implementation of recovery plans (where the negative effects of the pandemic were inevitable) were redefined. Some of the enterprises developed an integrated crisis management and business continuity plan in response to the COVID-19 pandemic. In the case of enterprise CON31, the objectives of such a plan included:

> to ensure an appropriate response to the occurrence of a crisis situation and to take adequate decisions and actions aimed at: restoring the execution of critical processes in the shortest possible time, preparing the companies and production facilities for prolonged interruptions in operations caused by internal and external factors remaining beyond their control and characterized by a low probability of occurrence and serious negative effects, as well as minimizing losses and negative consequences of the occurrence of a crisis situation.

In many enterprises, the synchronization of preventive and corrective actions resulted in the implementation of adequate crisis management procedures. Furthermore, focusing on ensuring the continuity of their business activities under the pandemic conditions, they also used: (1) the previously mentioned stress tests (characteristic of the FS sector), including cyclical tests and supervisory tests, (2) various scenarios of pandemic development and stress scenarios used to assess the risk of macroeconomic changes and verify the effectiveness of the implemented corrective actions.

Taking anti-crisis measures during a pandemic, the analysed companies followed the precautionary approach and the desire to achieve financial and operational stabilization, as well as to maintain their growth potential. For this purpose, as the results of our research indicate, it was common practice to develop prudential scenarios and contingency plans subject to cyclical revisions of assumptions and updates in order to adapt to current external conditions caused by the pandemic. Furthermore, to meet prudential and stabilization objectives, the examined enterprises often: (1) took advantage of business diversification (e.g. diversification of suppliers, sales channels, assortment/ service structures, sales markets), (2) searched for new sources of revenue and opportunities to reduce costs, (3) made every effort to retain their existing customer portfolio and (4) pursued a prudent investment policy that took into account the additional risks associated with the pandemic. They also dynamically implemented digitalization processes in order to maintain their operational potential and adapt it to the new conditions, all this to ensure continuity of sales and development work, as well as to provide conditions for returning to the path of growth and rebuilding their pre-pandemic revenue potential and market share. It is worth pointing out that we identified the actions and measures mentioned above in the representatives of all FS, CON and IT sectors.

The last of the top priorities established by the examined enterprises to build crisis resilience during the COVID-19 pandemic is maintaining the satisfaction of both internal and external stakeholders. To this end, many of the enterprises conducted extensive information, educational and training activities. Enterprises FS22 and CON2 are cases in point of many such practices observed by us. During the course of the pandemic the former implemented an electronic system of occupational development and training for employees, and the latter organized an e-learning platform dedicated to COVID-19 issues and security standards. Also, the vast majority of the companies introduced special procedures to protect the health of their employees, customers, suppliers and business partners. The comprehensiveness of the measures aimed at protecting stakeholders during the pandemic was observed in many of the companies under analysis. Enterprise CON9 described this comprehensiveness as follows:

> Already in the first quarter of 2020, we mobilised all our HR resources and competences to minimize the impact of COVID-19 on the organization with respect to our business operations, but above all our employees. The most important HR actions taken in the context of the fight against the pandemic:...we periodically communicated the results of analyses during security team meetings and – on an as needed basis – to individual units; we created training materials on an ongoing basis (e.g. about the status of an employee under quarantine/isolation) and practical instructions (e.g. how to open and use an Internet Patient Account); we supported communication with employees; we monitored the atmosphere within particular teams– HR Business Partners were in daily contact with employees of their assigned units/companies; we prepared an analysis of conditions for using government assistance programmes; we supported the Group companies in this respect; we launched a psychological helpline for employees in need of support. Our priority was to protect employment; being aware that despite the pandemic the labour market in the construction industry remained

very demanding, we focused on the optimal use of our employees' competences.

Moreover, many of the enterprises participating in the research monitored their stakeholders' reactions to the pandemic and renegotiated earlier contracts entered into with suppliers, contractors, clients, subcontractors and concerning, for example, office space rental, IT services, external consultancy services, sales, etc. Some of them (e.g. CON28, IT17) implemented additional measures to mitigate the risk of potential breach of contract terms as a result of changes in the economic situation, e.g. in the form of pandemic-related indemnifying clauses in newly concluded contracts. Enterprise IT14 described the need to renegotiate contracts due to the consequences of the pandemic as follows:

The Issuer's Management Board will endeavour to renegotiate already concluded contracts in which the supply of goods purchased outside Poland is an important element, and in the case of entering into new contracts of this type, it will introduce additional clauses protecting the Company against the risks related to financial instruments in the maximum possible way.

References

Ashby, S. (2011). Risk management and the global banking crisis: Lessons for insurance solvency regulation. *The Geneva Papers on Risk and Insurance. Issues and Practice*, 36(3), pp. 330–347.

Basak, B.D., Zhou Z. (2020). Diffusing coordination risk, *American Economic Review*, 110(1), pp. 271–297.

Crane, A., Matten, D. (2020). COVID-19 and the future of CSR research. *Journal of Management Studies*, 58(1), pp. 280–284.

Dawson, I.G.J. (2020). Taking responsibility: self-attribution for risk creation and its influence on the motivation to engage in risk management behaviours. *Journal of Risk Research*, 23(11), pp. 1440–1451.

Deloitte (2020). COVID-19: Managing supply chain risk and disruption. www2. deloitte.com/global/en/pages/risk/articles/covid-19-managing-supply-chain-risk-and-disruption.html (Access: 11.03.2022).

Engelhardt, L., White A. (2021). Pandemic response: Risk planning in times of a crisis. *American Journal of Management*, 21(4), pp. 16–30.

Ernst & Young (2020). Regulatory risk management for responding to COVID-19 pandemic (2020). https://assets.ey.com/content/dam/ey-sites/ey-com/en_in/topics/covid-19/regulatory-compliance-india-covid-19.pdf (Access: 7.03.2022).

Eylemer, S., Kirkpinar Özsoy, N. (2021). The European Union's response to COVID-19 as an existential threat. *International Journal of Contemporary Economics and Administrative Sciences*, 11(2), pp. 489–515.

International Monetary Fund (2020). Public Communication During a Financial Crisis. Monetary and Capital Markets. Special Series on COVID-19, www.imf.org/en/Publications/SPROLLs/covid19-special-notes (Access: 3.03.2022).

Jivaasha, D.D. (2021). Enterprise risk management culture – the testament of effective corporate governance. *Bimaquest*, 21(1), pp. 25–33.

Koekemoer, L., Beer, L.T. De, Govender, K., Brouwers, M. (2021). Leadership behaviour, team effectiveness, technological flexibility, work engagement and performance during COVID-19 lockdown: An exploratory study. *SA Journal of Industrial Psychology*, 47, pp. 1–9.

KPMG (2020). Global banking M&A outlook H2 2020 Report. https://home.kpmg/xx/en/home/insights/2020/07/covid-19-impact-on-banking-m-and-a-2020.html (Access: 11.02.2022).

Li, Y., Ashkanasy, N.M. (2019). Risk adaptation and emotion differentiation: An experimental study of dynamic decision-making. *Asia Pacific Journal of Management*, 36, pp. 219–243.

Marsh (2020). COVID-19: Evolving Insurance and Risk Management Implications. https://coronavirus.marsh.com/us/en/insights/research-and-briefings/covid-19-evolving-insurance-risk-management-implications.html (Access: 1.03.2022).

OECD (2020a). Regulatory Quality and COVID-19: Managing the Risks and Supporting the Recovery. www.oecd.org/regreform/regulatory-policy/Regulatory-Quality-and-Coronavirus%20-(COVID-19)-web.pdf (Access: 7.03.2022).

OECD (2020b). Policy options to support digitalization of Business Models during Covid-19: Annex. Report for the G20 Digital Economy Task Force. www.oecd.org/sti/policy-options-to-support-digitalization-of-business-models-during-covid-19-annex.pdf (Access: 13.03.2022).

Richter, C. (2013). Current developments in risk culture in financial organizations. *Journal of Economics and Management Research*, 3, pp. 75–86.

Rittenberg, L., Martens, F. (2012). Enterprise Risk Management. Understanding and Communicating Risk Appetite. The Committee of Sponsoring Organizations of the Treadway Commission (COSO), www.coso.org/Documents/ERM-Understanding-and-Communicating-Risk-Appetite.pdf (Access: 7.03.2022).

Saragih, S., Setiawan, S., Markus, T., Rhian, P. (2021). Benefits and challenges of telework during the Covid-19 pandemic. *International Journal of Business Studies*, 14(2), pp. 129–136.

Shengelia, T. (2021). Perspectives of small business development under the conditions of uncertainty caused by COVID pandemics. *Globalization and Business*, 11, pp. 77–82.

Wilke, A. (2020). Canadian employee safety considerations during the COVID-19 pandemic. *Plans & Trusts*, pp. 30–32.

7 Recommendations on the application of a new risk management maturity assessment model in enterprises

7.1 Participants in the assessment process

The selection of entities to participate in the risk management maturity assessment process is a crucial task determining its subsequent success or failure. If potential methodological errors are to be eliminated, it is necessary to involve participants representing a wide range of features and qualities. Two groups come to the fore: participants versed in risks occurring in various areas of activity and participants that are specialists in risk management. The former should represent all relevant functional areas, such as marketing, production, logistics, finance, administration, etc. The role of these individuals is primarily a qualitative assessment. On the other hand, from the perspective of quantifying maturity and allocating specific measures to it, people specializing in risk management are important. The latter group may include, for example:

- Employees holding the positions of Chief Risk Officer or Enterprise Risk Manager. According to research, about 39% of enterprises have such positions in their organizational structure (Mladenović, 2014). Individuals in these roles are highly trained and experienced in strategic risk management. In assessing maturity, they will therefore demonstrate an awareness of risks occurring across the whole organization and have an excellent background when it comes to assessing maturity from the perspective of resilience to crisis.
- Local and global assessment teams. This arrangement of participants can be used for large enterprises with global reach (Dobrin, 2021). Although seemingly unnecessary, the inclusion of a local perspective can nevertheless have a validating effect on assessment results.
- Strategic and operational managers. The participation of these executives makes a lot of sense. It is true that risk management

DOI: 10.4324/9781003330905-8

practices dedicated to strategic and operational management differ from each other, but maturity assessments should be holistic (Laurentiu, 2016).

- Stakeholders (e.g. suppliers) and industry experts (Claycamp, 2006). Čech and Januska (2020) justify the need for their participation in assessing the complexity of certain sectors such as the automotive sector. The presence of persons from outside the enterprise definitely enriches the assessment perspective and provides verification of internal optics and views.
- Risk management and audit committees, i.e. collegial bodies that are experienced in teamwork and, in addition, very competent in applying assessment and evaluation techniques (Abdullah et al., 2017).
- Compliance officers, i.e. individuals who are perfectly well versed in existing requirements of external and internal origin. Their contribution to maturity assessment comes from their knowledge of the degree to which the listed requirements are met.
- Representatives of consulting firms specialized in business analysis and, in recent years, often practising in the area of risk management. It is worth remembering that consultants have a broad perspective and knowledge of numerous sectors and companies. Their optics therefore allow maturity to be assessed in relative terms.

As maturity assessment is cyclical, the selection of assessors for the successive stages of maturity assessment may vary.

7.2 Methods of organizing the work of teams assessing risk management maturity

An assessment of risk management maturity is undoubtedly a complex and interdisciplinary task. It should therefore come as no surprise that a person working alone in this area will be doomed to failure.

What is relevant is this context is a number of nuances arising from sectoral specificities of enterprises and work organization methods. For example, in those industries where work is organized around projects (e.g. IT, construction), an approach combining the perspectives of different levels of management with that of the project function will be required in assessing risk management maturity (Yildiz et al., 2014). In particular, the aim of this type of integration is to obtain a reliable assessment and to capture divergent perceptions.

The shape of the work of teams assessing risk management maturity will be indirectly influenced by existing risk analysis techniques. One of the specifics of these techniques is teamwork formalization (Reis et al., 2021). It should therefore be recommended that the maturity assessment process include formal organizational and analytical techniques.

On the other hand, the example of risk management practices at the BMW Group shows that, in the case of multinational companies with a complex organizational structure and a multiplicity of different risks, it may be useful to segment the tasks at the initial stage of the maturity assessment process in order to be able to perform a synthesis of achieved results at the final stage (Dobrin, 2021). The initial assessment tasks can be performed by representatives of individual divisions or locations, and later a global team can integrate the partial results.

For the work of assessment teams, the support of top managers is extremely important. This support should range from legitimizing the work of assessment teams through providing them with necessary work conditions and resources to conducting joint reviews of assessment results (Sprčić et al., 2017).

As can be seen, therefore, there are no particular restrictions relating to the organization of work on maturity assessment. However, it is worth using proven and professional approaches, especially those developed in the area of risk management.

7.3 Integration of risk management maturity assessment with strategic management

Strategic management and risk management are interdependent management domains. An analytical approach to strategic management makes it possible to identify areas that need to be considered in terms of risk over a long time horizon. The issue of risk is one of the main subjects of analysis in holistic strategic management, determining the pursuit of leading strategic objectives. One of the strategic objectives of an enterprise should be to enable substantive cognition of the specificity of risks and the formation of a methodical approach to their analysis, which in turn should allow the enterprise to diagnose the probability of occurrence and the scope of risks, assess their potential impact on its functioning and ensure the continuity of its operations, even in crisis conditions (Urbanowska-Sojkin, 2012; Schroeder, 2014).

The leading stage of strategic management in an enterprise is the selection of a concept of its long-term development, in which the crucial elements are the identification, analysis, assessment and ongoing monitoring of risks. Precise risk assessments and risk minimization methods are particularly important for maintaining or strengthening an enterprise's competitive position, thus determining the effectiveness of the strategic management process. Furthermore, the strategic approach to risk should be based on the inference based on the knowledge of economic practices aimed at the development of enterprises in individual sectors in the face of escalating challenges of different nature (Goodfellow and Raynor, 2004; Urbanowska-Sojkin, 2013).

The intensity of interdependence between strategic management and risk management is also reflected in the development of the concept of Strategic Risk Management (SRM). The beginnings of the intensified worldwide implementation of this concept date back to the period after the global financial crisis of 2007. Before the crisis, the concept had been oriented towards shaping strategic objectives in adjustment to the risks arising from increased globalization processes (Clarke and Varma, 1999). After the global financial crisis, on the other hand, the main objective of the SRM concept became improving the processes of identification, assessment and management of risk factors that could cause significant economic losses and sometimes even lead to bankruptcy. The concept also finds an auxiliary application in crisis management, mainly in the process of recognizing the symptoms of crises and mitigating their negative consequences. The implementation of the SRM concept in an enterprise should therefore ultimately contribute to the development and implementation of strategic security solutions, the reduction of vulnerability to crises and the strengthening of readiness to change the business model in response to the occurring crisis situations (Calandro, 2015).

As described above, the relationship between risk management and strategic management in an enterprise justifies the need for ongoing monitoring of risk management maturity in strategic management processes, which maturity enterprises can measure using the model developed by us (described in Chapter 4). We considered the strategic dimension of risk management so important that one of the attributes of our model (A) is Strategy. In line with the principles of our model, we believe that the level of maturity of strategy-related risk management processes is determined by the following: (1) the degree to which uncertainty and leading risks are incorporated into the enterprise's strategy, (2) the identification of risks that are of strategic importance for the enterprise or its sector, (3) the characteristics of the leading strategy being pursued in the enterprise.

Another element influencing the effectiveness of strategic management is the formulation of strategies dedicated directly to risk management, i.e. a Risk Management Strategy (Gantz and Philpott, 2013) or fragmented strategies focusing on particular types of identified risks (Qu and Zhang, 2012; Chakraborty et al., 2021). A Risk Management

Strategy should set out detailed procedures by means of which risk managers and others responsible within the organizational structure for risk management processes identify, analyse, assess and monitor risks, as well as prepare responses for identified risks. Such a strategy should be a key determinant of corporate management decisions concerning risk anticipation, risk mitigation, risk prioritization, risk tolerance and risk acceptance criteria (Gantz and Philpott, 2013).

If the measurement and assessment of risk management maturity are to be effectively used in the enterprise's strategic management processes, it is extremely important to integrate the developed risk management strategy with other management strategies followed in the enterprise. The integration of these strategies should already take place at the levels of defining basic risk parameters, i.e. a risk profile, risk tolerance and risk appetite, as well as developing methods of risk protection. The result of such integration should be the inclusion of the approach that takes into account risks into all key phases of strategic management, i.e. building action and development plans, defining the business model, developing scenarios for dealing with various situations (including crises), monitoring the environment and introducing strategic changes.

A high level of risk management maturity can also be the first step on the way to building the enterprise's strategic resilience. Strategic resilience is particularly important in crisis situations, such as the COVID-19 pandemic. The pandemic crisis was a catalyst for many companies and business leaders to realize the immense value of resilience management. As it turned out in many cases, having contingency plans and early warning systems in the event of a crisis became the key to overcoming it or minimizing the severity of its negative consequences. An important element in the process of building strategic resilience is to be able to learn from past crises, and in particular to identify exposed gaps in resilience systems and to use this knowledge in the process of anticipating and preparing for future crises, thus consequently strengthening resilience. The most important features of strategic resilience are effectiveness and long-term sustainability. Crises in the operations of enterprises occur episodically, while strategic resilience should reflect the readiness for their occurrence at any time. Related to organization, resources and competences, outlays on building and maintaining strategic resilience are high, and their incurrence in non-crisis conditions may be a significant burden for the enterprise. However, for organizational resilience to have the qualities of strategic resilience, it must be sustained and improved even in safe conditions of functioning, when its tools are not directly needed (Natale et al., 2022).

Knowing the particular importance of developing crisis resilience in risk management processes, we included it in our model in the form of one of the attributes undergoing assessment, i.e. attribute (H) Crisis Resilience. We believe that an enterprise's risk management maturity is determined, among other things, by the degree of preparedness for potential crisis events, and in particular the previous development of resilience features based on the application of such concepts as culture of preparedness, business continuity and disaster resilience, as well as tools such as early warning systems, business continuity plans, disaster recovery plans, crisis scenarios and contingency plans (Jedynak and Bąk, 2021).

7.4 Conditions for the diffusion of the model in geographically and sectorally diversified enterprises

Our model for assessing risk management maturity (described in Chapter 4) is intended for application in enterprises functioning in any operating conditions, including crises. It allows any enterprise to assess the maturity of its activities vis-à-vis risk management. Our intention was to develop a measurement tool that has no geographical or sectoral implementation restrictions so that it can be used by any enterprise that needs to diagnose the status of its risk management processes. The conditions that have to be met in the maturity assessment process based on our model are presented in Sections 7.1 and 7.2.

We tested our multidimensional model on a group of enterprises representing three sectors (financial services, construction and IT) with very different characteristic features and operating conditions. The model allowed us to assess the risk management maturity of all examined enterprises, which confirms its applicability irrespective of any sectoral limitations.

We assessed the risk management maturity of the examined enterprises in relation to both the normal course of business (in the period before the COVID-19 pandemic) and crisis conditions (during the COVID-19 pandemic), which, in turn, confirms the practical usefulness of the model, regardless of the environmental conditions and the intensity of their interference with the enterprise's activities. Furthermore, our model can be used in assessing risk management maturity also during crises with other backgrounds.

Although we validated the model on a sample of Polish enterprises, its application is not limited to the Polish conditions of conducting business activities. The fact that a key part of our research process was to use the model to assess enterprises facing the challenge of risk management during a global pandemic crisis means that the model can be used by enterprises on a global scale. Indeed, the COVID-19 pandemic caused very similar effects on individual industries, regardless of the geographical location. This means that the pandemic experiences of enterprises in the financial services, construction and IT sectors in Poland were very similar to those of other companies belonging to the same sectors in other countries around the world.

The results of our in-depth research concerning the identification of specific changes related to the COVID-19 pandemic and reflected in the risk management maturity of the examined enterprises may therefore constitute important information for the modification of management processes for organizations operating worldwide and representing the sectors studied by us and others. We were able to determine what changes in risk characteristics had been caused by the pandemic, what modifying actions in the area of risk management it had forced enterprises to take and how it had influenced their current strategies, organizational cultures, roles and responsibilities in organizational structures, compliance systems and potential to utilize the developed crisis resilience.

Due to the fact that our research was conducted on a large sample of 107 enterprises, the obtained results are highly conclusive and can be used to formulate generalized opinions on and diagnoses of the impact of the COVID-19 pandemic on the activities and management processes of enterprises representing the sectors selected for our research.

Besides being an effective tool for enterprises to assess their progress in the area of risk management, our multidimensional model of risk management maturity can also be used in processes aimed at intra-organizational improvement. This is so because it allows the current status to be diagnosed on an ongoing basis, while simultaneously identifying management deficiencies in dealing with risks, and subsequently facilitating the programming of improvement actions. It can therefore be used in any phase of an enterprise's life cycle.

We also see the potential for our model to be used as a benchmarking tool in risk management processes. The experiences of the enterprises whose risk management maturity was assessed as 'superb' can constitute a valuable point of reference for other enterprises. The best companies develop mechanisms allowing them to make optimum decisions relating to risk management in both normal and crisis situations. The COVID-19 pandemic is one such situation when our model can be used as a benchmarking tool in risk management. Those companies analysed within the scope of our research that retained the highest level of risk management maturity despite the pressures of the pandemic may become forerunners of new standards for dealing with risks in crisis conditions. Such standards can subsequently be adapted by other companies, for example, to build resilience to further potential crisis threats.

Our research also showed that in many cases the COVID-19 pandemic had been a motivator for rapid, previously unplanned but effective management changes that improved individual enterprises' risk management maturity. It turned out that, despite not having had significant safety mechanisms in place before the pandemic, some of the examined companies, stimulated by the sudden and intense changes in many operational areas, were able to quickly develop defences that effectively protected them from the negative consequences of the pandemic. Such experiences may also be useful in the future for these and other enterprises.

However, the final conclusion of our research is that the companies performing the best in the face of the pandemic were those that already had a high level of risk management maturity before the crisis, i.e. those that, even under normal operating conditions, take steps to protect themselves against potential threats. A cyclical diagnosis of risk management maturity is therefore extremely important. It can be successfully performed in all enterprises by means of our multidimensional model of risk management maturity.

References

Abdullah, M., Shukor, Z.A., Rahmat, M.M. (2017). The influences of risk management committee and audit committee towards voluntary risk management disclosure. *Jurnal Pengurusan*, 50, pp. 1–20.

Calandro, J. (2015). A leader's guide to strategic risk management. *Strategy & Leadership*, 43(1), pp. 26–35.

Čech, M., Januška, M. (2020). Evaluation of risk management maturity in the Czech automotive industry: Model and methodology. *Amfiteatru Economic*, 22(55), pp. 824–845.

Chakraborty, G., Chandrashekhar, R.G., Balasubramanian, G. (2021). Measurement of extreme market risk: Insights from a comprehensive literature review. *Cogent Economics & Finance*, 9(1), 1920150.

Clarke, C.J., Varma, S. (1999). Strategic risk management: the new competitive edge. *Long Range Planning*, 32(4), pp. 414–424.

Claycamp, H.G. (2006). Rapid benefit-risk assessments: No escape from expert judgments in risk management. *Risk Analysis*, 26(1), pp. 147–156.

Dobrin, G. (2021). Analysis of risks and opportunities in the BMW Group. *Journal of Public Administration, Finance and Law*, 22, pp. 164–168.

Gantz, S.D., Philpott, D.R. (2013). *FISMA and the Risk Management Framework*. Chapter 13 Risk Management, pp. 329–365. www.elsevier.com/books/fisma-and-the-risk-management-framework/gantz/978-1-59749-641-4 (Access: 24.04.2022).

Goodfellow, J.L., Raynor, M.E. (2004). Managing strategic risk: a new partnership between the board and management. *Strategy & Leadership*, 32(5), pp. 45–47.

Jedynak, P., Bąk, S. (2021). *Risk Management in Crisis: Winners and Losers during the COVID-19 Pandemic*. London, New York: Routledge.

Laurentiu, M.R. (2016). The analysis of risk management process within management. *Annals of the „Constantin Brâncuşi" University of Târgu Jiu, Economy Series*, 5, pp. 101–105.

Mladenović, D. (2014). Chief Risk Officer & Enterprise Risk Management – How to Expect Unexpected. International Internet & Business Conference: Rovinj, Croatia.

Natale, A., Poppensieker, T., Thun, M. (2022). Senior executives at leading companies reveal their commitment to move from defensive risk management to a forward-looking stance based on strategic resilience. www.mckinsey.com/business-functions/risk-and-resilience/our-insights/from-risk-management-to-strategic-resilience (Access: 25.04.2022).

Qu, S., Zhang, Y. (2012). The Strategy of the Operational Risk Management: Connotations of it in Commercial Banks of China. Fifth International Conference on Business Intelligence and Financial Engineering, pp. 205–209. https://ieeexplore.ieee.org/document/6305112 (Access: 23.04.2022).

Reis, J., Özturk, Ş., Tülek, Z., Spencer, P. (2021). The COVID-19 pandemic, a risk management approach. *Turkish Journal of Neurology*, 27, pp. 1–5.

Schroeder, H. (2014). An art and science approach to strategic risk management. *Strategic Direction*, 30(4), pp. 28–30.

Sprčić, D.M., Kožul, A., Pecina, E. (2017). Managers' support – a key driver behind enterprise risk management maturity. *Zagreb International Review of Economics & Business*, 20, pp. 25–39.

Urbanowska-Sojkin, E. (2012). Ryzyko w zarządzaniu strategicznym przedsiębiorstwem: teoria i praktyka. *Zeszyty Naukowe Uniwersytetu Ekonomicznego w Poznaniu*, 235, pp. 35–53.

Urbanowska-Sojkin, E. (2013). *Ryzyko w wyborach strategicznych w przedsiębiorstwach*. Warszawa: PWE.

Yildiz, A.E., Dikmen, I., Birgonul, M.T. (2014). Using expert opinion for risk assessment: a case study of a construction project utilizing a risk mapping tool. *Procedia – Social and Behavioral Sciences*, 119, pp. 519–528.

Conclusions

One of the most important circumstances strongly verifying the efficiency of risk management systems and exposing their numerous imperfections is crisis situations. With regard to both risk management systems and risk management maturity models, crisis situations do not remain neutral, often necessitating the redefinition and reconstruction of either of them. Moreover, crises of significant scope, especially such as the COVID-19 pandemic (difficult to foresee, ignored or unpreventable) generate increased demand for the measurement and assessment of risk management maturity, taking into account the conditions imposed by a given situation.

The multidimensional model for the assessment of risk management maturity that we propose in this book constitutes a response to the identified increased demand for risk management maturity measurement in crisis situations. As part of the recommended maturity assessment process, we propose to assess eight attributes that we believe determine the level of risk management maturity. These attributes are: Strategy, Planning and goals, Culture, Standards and procedures, Processes, Roles and responsibilities, Compliance and Crisis resilience. We also developed five-point rating scales for all attributes, in the form of a Morphological Matrix. The next step was building a combined risk management maturity assessment scale that includes the ratings of all attributes. On this basis, we identified five levels of risk management maturity (fragmentary, basic, completed, professional, superb) and described the characteristic features of the risk management systems in place in the enterprises representing each of the identified maturity levels.

We validated the proposed risk management maturity assessment model on a sample of 107 enterprises representing the financial services, construction and IT sectors. We assessed their maturity for two

DOI: 10.4324/9781003330905-9

periods: the years 2018 (the pre-pandemic period) and 2020 (after the onset of the COVID-19 pandemic and during its course). The results of the conducted research allowed us to conclude that the crisis related to the COVID-19 pandemic had significantly affected the risk management systems functioning in the examined enterprises, which very often translated into changes in maturity assessments. An interesting conclusion of the research is also the fact that these changes were most often positive, i.e. improving risk management maturity, in relation to both the assessments of individual attributes and the final, comprehensive maturity assessment. This means that crisis situations stimulate companies to intensify processes aimed at protection against risk or against the negative consequences of its realization, which, in turn, is an important determinant of the shaping of resilience.

Our in-depth qualitative research also allowed us to determine what specific impact the COVID-19 pandemic situation had had on risk management maturity. It turned out that the most visible changes in the aftermath of the pandemic impacted the following attributes: Strategy, Culture, Roles and responsibilities, Compliance and Crisis resilience. We found that the identified changes were mainly influenced by contextual factors directly or indirectly related to the pandemic crisis. These caused significant transformations in risk artefacts and characteristics, scopes of responsibilities for risks, stakeholder relationships and priorities of the companies covered by the research. These transformations, in turn, resulted in specific actions taken by the enterprises, either to protect themselves from the negative effects of the crisis or to use the changes associated with it to improve their position.

The results of the research confirmed that our proposed multidimensional model of risk management maturity assessment could be applied in both normal business conditions and crisis situations. It can also be used in all types of enterprises, irrespective of any sectoral or geographical limitations. Our research also led us to conclude that the results of risk management maturity assessments were important factors influencing the organization of the strategic management process. In order to facilitate the use of our model by all interested entities, we also formulated recommendations for related organizational procedures, including assessment process participants and work organization methods to be followed by risk management maturity assessment teams.

Index

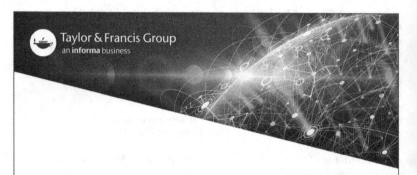

Printed in the United States
by Baker & Taylor Publisher Services

Printed in the United States
by Baker & Taylor Publisher Services